SOURCE
The Prentice Hall
ENGINEERING SOURCE

Introduction to Unix®

David I. Schwartz

The State University of New York–Buffalo

Prentice Hall
Upper Saddle River, NJ 07458

Library of Congress Cataloging-In-Publication Data

Schwartz, David I.
 Introduction to UNIX / David I. Schwartz
  p. cm.
 Includes bibliographical references and index.
 ISBN 0–13–095135-8
 1. Computer graphics. 2. Unix (Computer file).
 T385.D6327   1999
 604.2 ′0285′5369—dc21   98-50975
                                          CIP

Editor-in-chief: **MARCIA HORTON**
Acquisitions editor: **ERIC SVENDSEN**
Director of production and manufacturing: **DAVID W. RICCARDI**
Managing editor: **EILEEN CLARK**
Editorial/production supervision: **ROSE KERNAN**
Cover director: **JAYNE CONTE**
Creative director: **AMY ROSEN**
Marketing manager: **DANNY HOYT**
Manufacturing buyer: **PAT BROWN**
Editorial assistant: **GRIFFIN CABLE**

© 1999 by Prentice-Hall, Inc.
Upper Saddle River, New Jersey 07458

The author and publisher of this book have used their best efforts in
preparing this book. These efforts include the development, research,
and testing of the theories and programs to determine their effective-
ness. The author and publisher shall not be liable in any event for inci-
dental or consequential damages in connection with, or arising out of,
the furnishing, performance, or use of these programs.

Printed in the United States of America

10 9 8 7 6 5 4 3 2 1

ISBN 0-13-095135-8

Prentice-Hall International (UK) Limited, *London*
Prentice-Hall of Australia Pty. Limited, *Sydney*
Prentice-Hall Canada, Inc., *Toronto*
Prentice-Hall Hispanoamericana, S.A., *Mexico*
Prentice-Hall of India Private Limited, *New Delhi*
Prentice-Hall of Japan, Inc., *Tokyo*
Simon & Schuster Asia Pte., Ltd., *Singapore*
Editora Prentice-Hall do Brazil, Ltda., *Rio de Janeiro*

About ESource

The Challenge

Professors who teach the Introductory/First-Year Engineering course popular at most engineering schools have a unique challenge—teaching a course defined by a changing curriculum. The first-year engineering course is different from any other engineering course in that there is no real cannon that defines the course content. It is not like Engineering Mechanics or Circuit Theory where a consistent set of topics define the course. Instead, the introductory engineering course is most often defined by the creativity of professors and students, and the specific needs of a college or university each semester. Faculty involved in this course typically put extra effort into it, and it shows in the uniqueness of each course at each school.

Choosing a textbook can be a challenge for unique courses. Most freshmen require some sort of reference material to help them through their first semesters as a college student. But because faculty put such a strong mark on their course, they often have a difficult time finding the right mix of materials for their course and often have to go without a text, or with one that does not really fit. Conventional textbooks are far too static for the typical specialization of the first-year course. How do you find the perfect text for your course that will support your students educational needs, but give you the flexibility to maximize the potential of your course?

ESource—The Prentice Hall Engineering Source
http://emissary.prenhall.com/esource

Prentice Hall created ESource—The Prentice-Hall Engineering Source—to give professors the power to harness the full potential of their text and their freshman/first year engineering course. In today's technologically advanced world, why settle for a book that isn't perfect for your course? Why not have a book that has the exact blend of topics that you want to cover with your students?

More then just a collection of books, ESource is a unique publishing system revolving around the ESource website—http://emissary.prenhall.com/esource/. ESource enables you to put your stamp on your book just as you do your course. It lets you:

Control   You choose exactly what chapters or sections are in your book and in what order they appear. Of course, you can choose the entire book if you'd like and stay with the authors original order.

Optimize   Get the most from your book and your course. ESource lets you produce the optimal text for your students needs.

Customize You can add your own material anywhere in your text's presentation, and your final product will arrive at your bookstore as a professionally formatted text.

ESource Content

All the content in ESource was written by educators specifically for freshman/first-year students. Authors tried to strike a balanced level of presentation, one that was not either too formulaic and trivial, but not focusing heavily on advanced topics that most introductory students will not encounter until later classes. A developmental editor reviewed the books and made sure that every text was written at the appropriate level, and that the books featured a balanced presentation. Because many professors do not have extensive time to cover these topics in the classroom, authors prepared each text with the idea that many students would use it for self-instruction and independent study. Students should be able to use this content to learn the software tool or subject on their own.

While authors had the freedom to write texts in a style appropriate to their particular subject, all followed certain guidelines created to promote the consistency a text needs. Namely, every chapter opens with a clear set of objectives to lead students into the chapter. Each chapter also contains practice problems that tests a student's skill at performing the tasks they have just learned. Chapters close with extra practice questions and a list of key terms for reference. Authors tried to focus on motivating applications that demonstrate how engineers work in the real world, and included these applications throughout the text in various chapter openers, examples, and problem material. Specific Engineering and Science **Application Boxes** are also located throughout the texts, and focus on a specific application and demonstrating its solution.

Because students often have an adjustment from high school to college, each book contains several **Professional Success Boxes** specifically designed to provide advice on college study skills. Each author has worked to provide students with tips and techniques that help a student better understand the material, and avoid common pitfalls or problems first-year students often have. In addition, this series contains an entire book titled *Engineering Success* by Peter Schiavone of the University of Alberta intended to expose students quickly to what it takes to be an engineering student.

Creating Your Book

Using ESource is simple. You preview the content either on-line or through examination copies of the books you can request on-line, from your PH sales rep, or by calling(1-800-526-0485). Create an on-line outline of the content you want in the order you want using ESource's simple interface. Either type or cut and paste your own material and insert it into the text flow. You can preview the overall organization of the text you've created at anytime (please note, since this preview is immediate, it comes unformatted.), then press another button and receive an order number for your own custom book . If you are not ready to order, do nothing—ESource will save your work. You can come back at any time and change, re-arrange, or add more material to your creation. You are in control. Once you're finished and you have an ISBN, give it to your bookstore and your book will arrive on their shelves six weeks after the order. Your custom desk copies with their instructor supplements will arrive at your address at the same time.

To learn more about this new system for creating the perfect textbook, go to **http://emissary.prenhall.com/esource/**. You can either go through the on-line walkthrough of how to create a book, or experiment yourself.

Community

ESource has two other areas designed to promote the exchange of information among the introductory engineering community, the Faculty and the Student Centers. Created and maintained with the help of Dale Calkins, an Associate Professor at the University of Washington, these areas contain a wealth of useful information and tools. You can preview outlines created by other schools and can see how others organize their courses. Read a monthly article discussing important topics in the curriculum. You can post your own material and share it with others, as well as use what others have posted in your own documents. Communicate with our authors about their books and make suggestions for improvement. Comment about your course and ask for information from others professors. Create an on-line syllabus using our custom syllabus builder. Browse Prentice Hall's catalog and order titles from your sales rep. Tell us new features that we need to add to the site to make it more useful.

Supplements

Adopters of ESource receive an instructor's CD that includes solutions as well as professor and student code for all the books in the series. This CD also contains approximately **350 Powerpoint Transparencies** created by Jack Leifer—of University South Carolina—Aiken. Professors can either follow these transparencies as pre-prepared lectures or use them as the basis for their own custom presentations. In addition, look to the web site to find materials from other schools that you can download and use in your own course.

Titles in the ESource Series

About the Authors

No project could ever come to pass without a group of authors who have the vision and the courage to turn a stack of blank paper into a book. The authors in this series worked diligently to produce their books, provide the building blocks of the series.

Delores M. Etter is a Professor of Electrical and Computer Engineering at the University of Colorado. Dr. Etter was a faculty member at the University of New Mexico and also a Visiting Professor at Stanford University. Dr. Etter was responsible for the Freshman Engineering Program at the University of New Mexico and is active in the Integrated Teaching Laboratory at the University of Colorado. She was elected a Fellow of the Institute of Electrical and Electronic Engineers for her contributions to education and for her technical leadership in digital signal processing. IN addition to writing best-selling textbooks for engineering computing, Dr. Etter has also published research in the area of adaptive signal processing.

Sanford Leestma is a Professor of Mathematics and Computer Science at Calvin College, and received his Ph.D from New Mexico State University. He has been the long time co-author of successful textbooks on Fortran, Pascal, and data structures in Pascal. His current research interests are in the areas of algorithms and numerical compuitation.

Larry Nyhoff is a Professor of Mathematics and Computer Science at Calvin College. After doing bachelors work at Calvin, and Masters work at Michigan, he received a Ph.D. from Michigan State and also did graduate work in computer science at Western Michigan. Dr. Nyhoff has taught at Calvin for the past 34 years—mathematics at first and computer science for the past several years. He has co-authored several computer science textbooks since 1981 including titles on Fortran and C++, as well as a brand new title on Data Structures in C++.

Acknowledgments: We express our sincere appreciation to all who helped in the preparation of this module, especially our acquisitions editor Alan Apt, managing editor Laura Steele, development editor Sandra Chavez, and production editor Judy Winthrop. We also thank Larry Genalo for several examples and exercises and Erin Fulp for the Internet address application in Chapter 10. We appreciate the insightful review provided by Bart Childs. We thank our families—Shar, Jeff, Dawn, Rebecca, Megan, Sara, Greg, Julie, Joshua, Derek, Tom, Joan; Marge, Michelle, Sandy, Lori, Michael—for being patient and understanding. We thank God for allowing us to write this text.

Mark Dix began working with AutoCAD in 1985 as a programmer for CAD Support Associates, Inc. He helped design a system for creating estimates and bills of material directly from AutoCAD drawing databases for use in the automated conveyor industry. This system became the basis for systems still widely in use today. In 1986 he began collaborating with Paul Riley to create AutoCAD training materials, combining Riley's background in industrial design and training with Dix's background in writing, curriculum development, and programming. Dix and Riley have created tutorial and teaching methods for every AutoCAD release since Version 2.5. Mr. Dix has a Master of Arts in Teaching from Cornell University and a Masters of Education from the University of Massachusetts. He is currently the Director of Dearborn Academy High School in Arlington, Massachusetts.

Paul Riley is an author, instructor, and designer specializing in graphics and design for multimedia. He is a founding partner of CAD Support Associates, a contract service and professional training organization for computer-aided design. His 15 years of business experience and 20 years of teaching experience are supported by degrees in education and computer science. Paul has taught AutoCAD at the University of Massachusetts at Lowell and is presently teaching AutoCAD at Mt. Ida College in Newton, Massachusetts. He has developed a program, <u>Computer-Aided Design for Professionals</u> that is highly regarded by corporate clients and has been an ongoing success since 1982.

 **David I. Schwartz** is a Lecturer at SUNY-Buffalo who teaches freshman and first-year engineering, and has a Ph.D from SUNY-Buffalo in Civil Engineering. Schwartz originally became interested in Civil engineering out of an interest in building grand structures, but has also pursued other academic interests including artificial intelligence and applied mathematics. He became interested in Unix and Maple through their application to his research, and eventually jumped at the chance to teach these subjects to students. He tries to teach his students to become incremental learners and encourages frequent practice to master a subject, and gain the maturity and confidence to tackle other subjects independently. In his spare time, Schwartz is an avid musician and plays drums in a variety of bands.

Acknowledgments: I would like to thank the entire School of Engineering and Applied Science at the State University of New York at Buffalo for the opportunity to teach not only my students, but myself as well; all my EAS140 students, without whom this book would not be possible—thanks for slugging through my lab packets; Andrea Au, Eric Svendsen, and Elizabeth Wood at Prentice Hall for advising and encouraging me as well as wading through my blizzard of e-mail; Linda and Tony for starting the whole thing in the first place; Rogil Camama, Linda Chattin, Stuart Chen, Jeffrey Chottiner, Roger Christian, Anthony Dalessio, Eugene DeMaitre, Dawn Halvorsen, Thomas Hill, Michael Lamanna, Nate "X" Patwardhan, Durvejai Sheobaran, "Able" Alan Somlo, Ben Stein, Craig Sutton, Barbara Umiker, and Chester "JC" Zeshonski for making this book a reality; Ewa Arrasjid, "Corky" Brunskill, Bob Meyer, and Dave Yearke at "the Department Formerly Known as ECS" for all their friendship, advice, and respect; Jeff, Tony, Forrest, and Mike for the interviews; and, Michael Ryan and Warren Thomas for believing in me.

 **Ronald W. Larsen** is an Associate Professor in Chemical Engineering at Montana State University, and received his Ph.D from the Pennsylvania State University. Larsen was initially attracted to engineering because he felt it was a serving profession, and because engineers are often called on to eliminate dull and routine tasks. He also enjoys the fact that engineering rewards creativity and presents constant challenges. Larsen feels that teaching large sections of students is one of the most challenging tasks he has ever encountered because it enhances the importance of effective communication. He has drawn on a two year experince teaching courses in Mongolia through an interpreter to improve his skills in the classroom. Larsen sees software as one of the changes that has the potential to radically alter the way engineers work, and his book Introduction to Mathcad was written to help young engineers prepare to be productive in an ever-changing workplace.

Acknowledgments: To my students at Montana State University who have endured the rough drafts and typos, and who still allow me to experiment with their classes— my sincere thanks.

 **Peter Schiavone** is a professor and student advisor in the Department of Mechanical Engineering at the University of Alberta. He received his Ph.D. from the University of Strathclyde, U.K. in 1988. He has authored several books in the area of study skills and academic success as well as numerous papers in scientific research journals.

Before starting his career in academia, Dr. Schiavone worked in the private sector for Smith's Industries (Aerospace and Defence Systems Company) and Marconi Instruments in several different areas of engineering including aerospace, systems and software engineering. During that time he developed an interest in engineering research and the applications of mathematics and the physical sciences to solving real-world engineering problems.

His love for teaching brought him to the academic world. He founded the first Mathematics Resource Center at the University of Alberta: a unit designed specifically to teach high school students the necessary survival skills in mathematics and the physical sciences required for first-year engineering. This led to the Students' Union Gold Key award for outstanding contributions to the University and to the community at large.

Dr. Schiavone lectures regularly to freshman engineering students, high school teachers, and new professors on all aspects of engineering success, in particular, maximizing students' academic performance. He wrote the book *Engineering Success* in order to share with you the *secrets of success in engineering study*: the most effective, tried and tested methods used by the most successful engineering students.

Acknowledgments: I'd like to acknowledge the contributions of: Eric Svendsen, for his encouragement and support; Richard Felder for being such an inspiration; the many students who shared their experiences of first-year engineering—both good and bad; and finally, my wife Linda for her continued support and for giving me Conan.

Scott D. James is a staff lecturer at Kettering University (formerly GMI Engineering & Management Institute) in Flint, Michigan. He is currently pursuing a Ph.D. in Systems Engineering with an emphasis on software engineering and computer-integrated manufacturing. Scott decided on writing textbooks after he found a void in the books that were available. "I really wanted a book that showed how to do things in good detail but in a clear and concise way. Many of the books on the market are full of fluff and force you to dig out the really important facts." Scott decided on teaching as a profession after several years in the computer industry. "I thought that it was really important to know what it was like outside of

academia. I wanted to provide students with classes that were up to date and provide the information that is really used and needed."

Acknowledgments: Scott would like to acknowledge his family for the time to work on the text and his students and peers at Kettering who offered helpful critique of the materials that eventually became the book.

David C. Kuncicky is a native Floridian. He earned his Baccalaureate in psychology, Master's in computer science, and Ph.D. in computer science from Florida State University. Dr. Kuncicky is the Director of Computing and Multimedia Services for the FAMU-FSU College of Engineering. He also serves as a faculty member in the Department of Electrical Engineering. He has taught computer science and computer engineering courses for the past 15 years. He has published research in the areas of intelligent hybrid systems and neural networks. He is actively involved in the education of computer and network system administrators and is a leader in the area of technology-based curriculum delivery.

Acknowledgments: Thanks to Steffie and Helen for putting up with my late nights and long weekends at the computer. Thanks also to the helpful and insightful technical reviews by the following people: Jerry Ralya, Kathy Kitto of Western Washington University, Avi Singhal of Arizona State University, and Thomas Hill of the State University of New York at Buffalo. I appreciate the patience of Eric Svendsen and Rose Kernan of Prentice Hall for gently guiding me through this project. Finally, thanks to Dean C.J. Chen for providing continued tutelage and support.

Mark Horenstein is an Associate Professor in the Electrical and Computer Engineering Department at Boston University. He received his Bachelors in Electrical Engineering in 1973 from Massachusetts Institute of Technology, his Masters in Electrical Engineering in 1975

from University of California at Berkeley, and his Ph.D. in Electrical Engineering in 1978 from Massachusetts Institute of Technology. Professor Horenstein's research interests are in applied electrostatics and electromagnetics as well as microelectronics, including sensors, instrumentation, and measurement. His research deals with the simulation, test, and measurement of electromagnetic fields. Some topics include electrostatics in manufacturing processes, electrostatic instrumentation, EOS/ESD control, and electromagnetic wave propagation.

Professor Horenstein designed and developed a class at Boston University, which he now teaches entitled Senior Design Project (ENG SC 466). In this course, the student gets real engineering design experience by working for a virtual company, created by Professor Horenstein, that does real projects for outside companies—almost like an apprenticeship. Once in "the company" (Xebec Technologies), the student is assigned to an engineering team of 3-4 persons. A series of potential customers are recruited, from which the team must accept an engineering project. The team must develop a working prototype deliverable engineering system that serves the need of the customer. More than one team may be assigned to the same project, in which case there is competition for the customer's business.

Acknowledgements: Several individuals contributed to the ideas and concepts presented in Design Principles for Engineers. The concept of the Peak Performance design competition, which forms a cornerstone of the book, originated with Professor James Bethune of Boston University. Professor Bethune has been instrumental in conceiving of and running Peak Performance each year and has been the inspiration behind many of the design concepts associated with it. He also provided helpful information on dimensions and tolerance. Several of the ideas presented in the book, particularly the topics on brainstorming and teamwork, were gleaned from a workshop on engineering design help bi-annually by Professor Charles Lovas of Southern Methodist University. The principles of estimation were derived in part from a freshman engineering problem posed by Professor Thomas Kincaid of Boston University.

I would like to thank my family, Roxanne, Rachel, and Arielle, for giving me the time and space to think about and write this book. I also appreciate Roxanne's inspiration and help in identifying examples of human/machine interfaces.

Dedicated to Roxanne, Rachel, and Arielle

Charles B. Fleddermann is a professor in the Department of Electrical and Computer Engineering at the University of New Mexico in Albuquerque, New Mexico. He is a third generation engineer—his grandfather was a civil engineer and father an aeronautical engineer—so "engineering was in my genetic makeup." The genesis of a book on engineering ethics was in the ABET requirement to incorporate ethics topics into the undergraduate engineering curriculum. "Our department decided to have a one-hour seminar course on engineering ethics, but there was no book suitable for such a course." Other texts were tried the first few times the course was offered, but none of them presented ethical theory, analysis, and problem solving in a readily accessible way. "I wanted to have a text which would be concise, yet would give the student the tools required to solve the ethical problems that they might encounter in their professional lives."

Reviewers

ESource benefited from a wealth of reviewers who on the series from its initial idea stage to its completion. Reviewers read manuscripts and contributed insightful comments that helped the authors write great books. We would like to thank everyone who helped us with this project.

Concept Document

Naeem Abdurrahman- University of Texas, Austin
Grant Baker- University of Alaska, Anchorage
Betty Barr- University of Houston
William Beckwith- Clemson University
Ramzi Bualuan- University of Notre Dame
Dale Calkins- University of Washington
Arthur Clausing- University of Illinois at Urbana-Champaign
John Glover- University of Houston
A.S. Hodel- Auburn University
Denise Jackson- University of Tennessee, Knoxville
Kathleen Kitto- Western Washington University
Terry Kohutek- Texas A&M University
Larry Richards- University of Virginia
Avi Singhal- Arizona State University
Joseph Wujek- University of California, Berkeley
Mandochehr Zoghi- University of Dayton

Books

Stephen Allan- Utah State University
Naeem Abdurrahman - University of Texas Austin
Anil Bajaj- Purdue University
Grant Baker - University of Alaska - Anchorage
Betty Barr - University of Houston

William Beckwith - Clemson University
Haym Benaroya- Rutgers University
Tom Bledsaw- ITT Technical Institute
Tom Bryson- University of Missouri, Rolla
Ramzi Bualuan - University of Notre Dame
Dan Budny- Purdue University
Dale Calkins - University of Washington
Arthur Clausing - University of Illinois
James Devine- University of South Florida
Patrick Fitzhorn - Colorado State University
Dale Elifrits- University of Missouri, Rolla
Frank Gerlitz - Washtenaw College
John Glover - University of Houston
John Graham - University of North Carolina-Charlotte
Malcom Heimer - Florida International University
A.S. Hodel - Auburn University
Vern Johnson- University of Arizona
Kathleen Kitto - Western Washington University
Robert Montgomery- Purdue University
Mark Nagurka- Marquette University
Ramarathnam Narasimhan- University of Miami
Larry Richards - University of Virginia
Marc H. Richman - Brown University
Avi Singhal-Arizona State University
Tim Sykes- Houston Community College
Thomas Hill- SUNY at Buffalo
Michael S. Wells - Tennessee Tech University
Joseph Wujek - University of California - Berkeley
Edward Young- University of South Carolina
Mandochehr Zoghi - University of Dayton

Contents

6   FILE MANAGEMENT

7   UNIX TOOLS AND UTILITIES

8   ADVANCED UNIX

APPENDIX A: SYMBOL NAMES   102

APPENDIX B: WINDOW SYSTEMS   103

APPENDIX C: TEXT EDITORS   107

APPENDIX D: E-MAIL PROGRAMS   110

http://emissary.prenhall.com/esource/

1

Computing with Unix

1.1 COMPUTER BASICS

What is a computer? Why do we need computers? How do we use them? This section provides some answers to these questions, as well as a bit of background on computing and computers.

1.1.1 Computers Are Tools

Computers are tools, devices that assist and ease cumbersome and seemingly impossible tasks. Not only do tools consist of physical devices, but instructions and methods. Such abstract tools instruct us how to accomplish a goal—solving mathematical problems, for example, and often, no physical tools other than a human brain, some paper, and pencils are necessary. So, do we *need* computers?

Some people still insist that dependency on computers turns our brains to mush. Without computers, though, many tasks would require countless hours of hand calculations, and, in any case, no one should completely depend on computers. Never blindly trust a computer's output. Always check your input. Remember GIGO: garbage in, garbage out. Use traditional pencil-and-paper analysis on simplified engineering models to check computer results. Always remember that computers are incredibly useful tools that require diligence and understanding.

1.1.2 History of Computing

Merriam Webster's Collegiate Dictionary defines a *computer* as a "programmable electronic device that can store, retrieve, and process data." Throughout the millennia, people have used tools to assist with computations. For instance, a sundial marks the passage of time by tracking shadows, and an abacus performs arithmetic with sliding

OBJECTIVES

After reading this chapter, you should be able to:

- Discuss background and philosophy of computers
- Overview basics of computer hardware and software
- Illustrate features and advantages of using the Unix operating system

beads. Throughout the late nineteenth and twentieth centuries, computing technology rapidly improved, until finally, the invention of the electronic computer chip began the microcomputer revolution in the 1970s. Computer technology constantly changes and improves.

1.1.3 Computer Classifications

Computers are generally classified into four categories: supercomputers, mainframes, minicomputers, and microcomputers. Very large and expensive supercomputers typically handle very complex problems in high-level engineering and scientific enterprises. Mainframe computers supply services for many users in industry and academia. Mainframes typically control processes for other computers in a network. Powerful, stand-alone minicomputers rival the power and speed of mainframes. Scientific research and engineering analysis often use minicomputers as shown in Figure 1.1. Smaller mainframes, or minicomputers, are often referred to as *workstations*. Microcomputers are even smaller and often called personal computers. These computers are typically either connected to mainframes or exist as stand-alone machines in homes and offices.

1.1.4 Computer Components and Usage

The physical components that comprise computers are called **hardware**. The computer's "intelligence" comes from **software**, instructions that control and instruct the hardware. Software that is created to perform specific tasks is called a *program*.

Figure 1.1.   Unix at Work (Courtesy of Sun Microsystems, Inc.)

1.2 COMPUTER HARDWARE

The great variety of computers share similar features. In general, five main components classify computer hardware: the processor and memory, and devices for input, output, and storage.

- *Input:* Devices such as keyboards, mice, scanners, or other data-acquistion systems enter instructions and other information.
- *Processor:* The central processing unit (CPU) resembles the brain of the computer. The CPU interprets instructions entered by input devices. Signals sent to other hardware components implement these instructions.
- *Memory:* The computer stores instructions and data in storage cells for access by the CPU. Internal memory usually splits between random-access memory (RAM) and read-only memory (ROM). RAM provides temporary space for reading and writing information required by programs. ROM stores permanent programs and other information supplied by the manufacturer.
- *Storage:* External devices such as floppy disks, CD-ROMs, and hard drives store electronic information. Programs stored in such devices must be loaded into internal memory before the CPU can perform instructed tasks.
- *Output:* The most common output device is the video display terminal (VDT), often referred to as the *monitor.* Much like cinematic film, the image constantly refreshes faster than the human eye can perceive. Another form of output is hardcopy such as printouts on paper.

Figure 1.2 depicts these components in a typical configuration: A keyboard or mouse enters, or inputs, commands. The CPU then processes these instructions and usually displays results on the monitor, or perhaps stores results on a medium such as a floppy disk.

1.3 COMPUTER SOFTWARE

Without programs, the CPU contains bunches of inert circuits and chips. The CPU requires "knowledge," or instructions, in order to process input into useful output. Although computers are not really intelligent, software imparts a sense of life to computer hardware.

Figure 1.2.   Example Unix Workstation

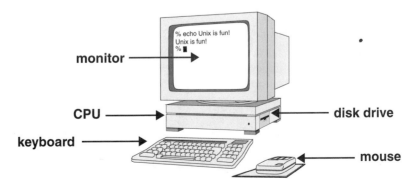

1.3.1 Bits, Bytes, and All That

Often, movies glorify computers. How many times have you seen a character enter a command like "find password," and, after a few moments, have the computer report, "secret password found"? Be glad that cracking into someone's account is not so simple.

How do real computers understand instructions? Most computers today are digital. Digital computers convert and store information with the digits 0 and 1—*binary digits*, or just **bits**. Bits form the smallest component of computer memory. A group of eight bits makes up a **byte**. Jargon such as *"megs"* or *"gigs"* refers to larger chunks of memory, as shown in Table 1-1.

1.3.2 Programs

Everyone follows instructions every day—baking a cake requires following a recipe to produce a tasty dessert. Starting a car requires a sequence of steps, without which you will be seeking other modes of transportation. Computer programs are also instructions, written in a programming language that the CPU understands. Some programs, such as file management software, are internally stored. Others are loaded into memory from external storage devices.

Common programs that perform tasks such as word processing, financial analysis, number crunching, and others are called "application software." Application software, or just applications, are typically purchased from independent vendors. Many software engineers even develop in-house programs for companies to use.

Programs designed to help people use computers and applications are called *system software.* Such programs include utilities for common tasks such as file management and electronic mail. System software that specifically controls the internal workings of the computer is called an **operating system**.

1.3.3 Operating Systems

The CPU uses the operating system (**OS**) to control all computer functions. When you turn on a computer, the OS is loaded into main memory. The OS is typically activated with typed commands or graphical interfaces, and all instructions from input are then interpreted and acted upon by the OS. Because different processes require different memory demands, the OS must act as referee and properly allocate resources. The OS also controls how applications transfer data between main memory and output.

1.3.4 Graphical User Interface

Originally, computers had unfriendly interfaces, such as monochrome monitors and teletype machines. Programming even required punchcards for input! Eventually, windows-based **graphical user interface** (**GUI**, pronounced *goo-ee*) computers were developed. GUI-oriented software presents an interface of pull-down menus and point-and-click mouse operations inside windows, which activate the actual operating system. GUIs tend to avoid text-based command entry in order to provide a friendlier environment. Refer to Appendix B for more information on typical Unix GUIs.

TABLE 1-1 Computer Memory Sizes

JARGON	ACTUAL VALUES (BYTES)
K = kilobyte	2^{10} (1,024)
M = megabyte	2^{20} (1,048,576)
G = gigabyte	2^{30} (1,073,741,824)
T = terabyte	2^{40} (1,099,511,627,776)

1.4 THE UNIX OPERATING SYSTEM

Unix (pronounced *you-nix*) is an operating system that is gaining popularity beyond traditional academic and scientific-institution research. In fact, many large corporations employ Unix as their standard OS. Even the Internet and Unix share common background, as discussed in Chapter 4. This section presents some background and reasons for using Unix.

1.4.1 History of Unix

Unix did not start as a multimillion-dollar research project sponsored by some large, multinational corporation. Nor did Unix hide from prying eyes as a supersecret military project. Rather, Unix was born in 1969 in Bell Labs as a better way to run Space Travel, an astronomical-simulation program—yes, Unix was developed to play a *computer game.*

Ken Thompson, a developer of Unix, had become frustrated with running Space Travel on a Multics (*mult*iplexed *i*nformation and *c*omputing *s*ystem) computer. He eventually moved the program to another computer in the corner of his lab so that he could experiment. By 1973, after many revisions in assembly code, Ken Thompson and Dennis Ritchie rewrote Unix in C, a language specifically developed for Unix. *Unix,* in fact, is a pun on *Multics:* just replace "*multi*plexed" with "*uni*plexed."

Eventually, AT&T, the owner of Bell Labs, released Unix to educational institutions, but without any support. Then, since the source code was publicly available, computer programmers began enhancing Unix's capabilities. Programmers at the University of California at Berkeley, for example, added many features that eventually became standardized in Berkeley Software Distribution (BSD) and other versions of Unix. AT&T retained its own version, too, one that incorporated features developed by others and was eventually released as System V Release 4 (SVR4).

1.4.2 Unix Variants

Through the years since Thompson and Ritchie's original creation, different versions of Unix, both commercial and free, have cropped up. (Some of the more significant major versions are listed in Table 1-2.) At present, there two main varieties of Unix: SVR4 and BSD. Standardized "standards" have been proposed, such as Portable Operating System Interface for Computer Environments (POSIX), System V Interface Definition (SVID), and X/Open. X/Open currently owns the brand name "Unix."

TABLE 1-2 Major Unix Variants

VERSION	DESCRIPTION
AIX	IBM's Advanced Interactive Executive OS
BSD	University of California's Berkeley Software Distribution
HP-UX	Hewlett-Packard's Unix
IRIX	Silicon Graphics's Unix
Linux	Linus Torvalds's Unix—very popular among personal computer users
Mach	Carnegie Mellon's version—adapted by OSF/1
OSF/1	Open Software Foundation's attempt to standardize Unix
Solaris	Sun Microsystems's current and very powerful version of Unix, based on SVR4
SunOS	Sun Microsystems's version of Unix that is being replaced by Solaris
System V	AT&T's version of Unix, also called System V Release 4 or SVR4
XENIX	Microsoft's Unix—also called Santa Cruz Operation (SCO) Unix. UnixWare is also owned by SCO

1.4.3 Why Unix?

Students often ask why we need to learn Unix. After all, what about those "other" operating systems? There is, of course, the simple answer: "because that's what we use here." However, this answer begs the question of *why* Unix in the first place.

First, forget the notion that any window environment is an OS. GUIs shield users from the OS. Unfortunately, inexperienced or unknowledgeable users can still get burned if a GUI "crashes,"[1] and knowing text-based commands helps diagnose and fix computer problems. Even with well-oiled GUIs, however, experienced users eventually tire of tedious point-and-click mouse operations. Have you ever wondered why most GUI programs include keyboard shortcuts? Text-based command entry often *improves* efficiency.

Originally, Unix was designed for computers with limited internal memory. *Every* character counted. For example, why use "copy" when "cp" suffices? Unix commands were created to be lean and mean, to quickly perform a wide variety of tasks. Granted, many commands appear somewhat cryptic. But despite that, when rating an OS, look beneath glittery window interfaces. Unix has many advantages to offer:

- *Openness:* The source code for Unix is publicly available. Developers can readily adapt utilities to suit needs, and often, standard releases globally adapt Unix-variants.
- *Utilities:* A multitude of programs arrive standard, or "bundled," with most versions of Unix. A variety of commercial and public-domain software is also available.
- *Portability:* Virtually every kind of computer supports Unix.
- *Multiuser:* Unix can simultaneously handle many users running different programs.
- *Multitasking:* A user can run different programs simultaneously in Unix.
- *Networking:* Unix allows computers to connect and share information. In fact, Unix protocols, or methods of transferring information, form the basis of the Internet.
- *Prevalence:* Workstations that employ Unix help solve many complex engineering and science problems.

Unix is typically taught and used as a text-based OS. However, many Unix GUIs are available, including X Windows, Common Desktop Environment, and others. These GUIs contain essentially the same features of other GUIs for other operating systems. But before rushing to use a GUI, consider that a good engineer or scientist strives to understand the theory behind her or his tools. Knowing the guts of Unix will help you customize your commands later on and better understand a GUI. Granted, using a cryptic, text-based OS might seem like taking a step backward, but in light of the power that Unix offers, moving backward will help you leap forward.

APPLICATION: UNIX AND YOUR CAREER

How will learning Unix help your career? I asked four engineering and science professionals about their Unix experience. Here's some advice they have for students:

- Jeffrey Chottiner, Ford product-design engineer; designs engines: Recent projects include a cranktrain for a highly efficient all-

[1] There are even more colorful expressions for computer software failures. Such vulgar—and often humorous—terminology shall be left for the reader to discover in the course of her or his career.

aluminum diesel engine in a hybrid electric vehicle. Jeff says that "Unix is like coffee. Without it I'm useless." Besides using Unix to edit "finite element decks" (structural-analysis input-data files) and organize his many project files, he uses FTP (File Transfer Protacol, a Unix Internet program) to immediately obtain "vital engine-performance data from Germany." Unix features such as multitasking have improved his efficiency. "Unix saves me and Ford time and money."

- Anthony Dalessio, RF/microwave engineer; designs circuits such as filters, amplifiers, and power dividers for use in the cellular, paging, and public-safety communication systems. Tony has used Unix for over five years. When he worked at Wright Patterson Air Force Base, "all the microwave-design tools in the avionics directorate were running on Unix workstations." He is also a Linux expert and suggests that students download Linux for their PCs. "Several programs for electrical engineering, such as Spice [a circuit simulator] and Magic [for Very Large Scale Integration—VLSI design] have been ported to Linux." Better yet, "using Linux sure beats going to a computer lab at 2 A.M. to get an open terminal."

- Forrest Hoffman, computer specialist—technical; designs and implements scientific computer models. Forrest has been using Unix for scientific software development, visualization, and communications for nearly ten years. His familiarity with the Unix operating system allowed him to develop a World Wide Web site and a commodity parallel-computer cluster built from PCs running Linux at Oak Ridge National Laboratory. "Unix is the perfect environment for scientific computing," he states. Most of the best scientific analysis and prediction software runs under Unix, "and the source code is usually available, so anyone can modify it for their own use." For parallel computing, Linux, GNU compilers and tools, and the Parallel Virtual Machine (PVM) and Message Passing Interface (MPI) message-passing libraries running on PCs offer the lowest-cost solutions, because "All the software is free."

- Michael Lamanna, civil- and software-engineering research scientist; researching Internet-based software and expert systems. Mike has used Unix for eight years for school and his research. His projects include remote structural-monitoring applications. How does he use Unix? "E-mail, and the world's greatest editor/environment/everything: Emacs [a popular Unix text editor and programming-development environment]!"

1.5 UNIX BASICS

Even today, software developers try to abide by original Unix philosophies dictating that commands should be simple, general, and adaptable. Not all Unix commands and utilities follow these principles exactly, but Unix has retained the general flavor of its origins. This section provides an overview of the main components of Unix.

1.5.1 Software Layers

Between the user and the computer hardware lie three layers of the Unix OS, as shown in Figure 1.3. The outermost layer, the **shell**, reads and interprets your commands. (Essential commands are demonstrated throughout the entire book.) Not all versions of Unix use the same shells, and often, a few different shells may be available on any given system. Furthermore, some commands even differ from shell to shell. The **resident modules** compose the next layer and perform important services such as Input/Output and process control. The innermost layer, the **kernel**, directs the hardware to perform your commands.

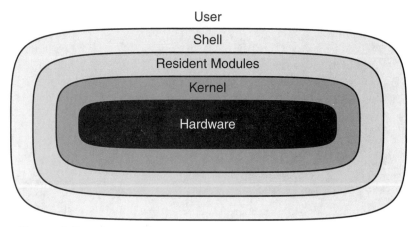

Figure 1.3. Unix Layers

1.5.2 File System

Scientists and engineers are frequently concerned with data, and managing it—how to enter it, where to put it, and how to use it are crucial tasks. A *file system* provides methods for doing so.

Tasks such as report writing, programming, and analysis generate heaps of electronic information that *files* store. In time, storing groups of related files inside *directories* will better organize your data. Directories, in turn, are arranged in hierarchical structures often known as *directory trees,* illustrated in Figure 1.4. Think of a directory tree as a filing cabinet: directories would be drawers containing files as contents. But Unix would be a very large filing cabinet! With Unix, very many directories may store other directories, and all may house their own files as well.

Figure 1.4. Example Directory Tree

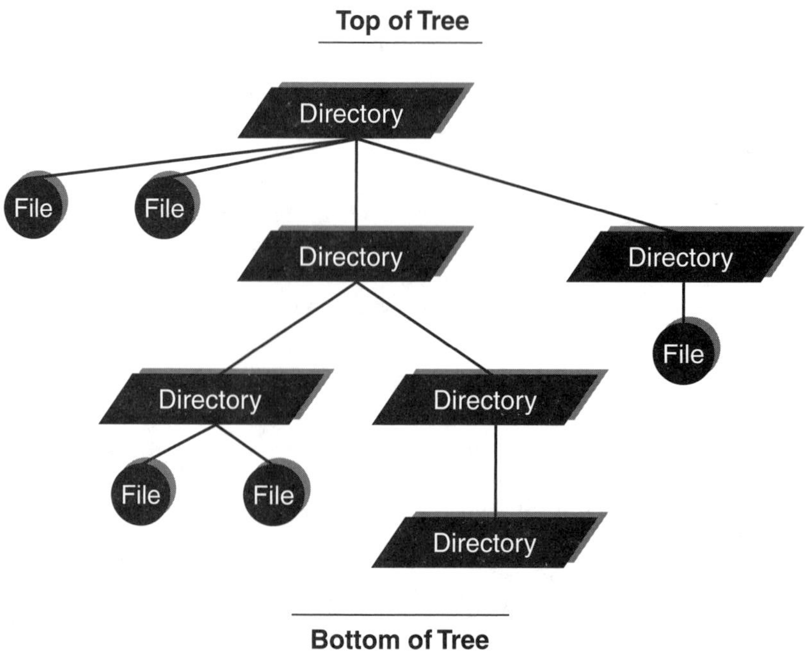

Top of Tree

Bottom of Tree

1.5.3 Utilities

Hundreds of separate Unix programs arrive built-in with the OS, and many system administrators further enhance their computing environments with public-domain "freeware," programs that are freely (or at least cheaply) distributed. Just about every possible task is covered by one, if not more, programs. Moreover, additional commercial software is available.

1.5.4 Unix GUIs

Unix is primarily text-based, but GUIs are available for it. The X Windows system developed by Massachusetts Institute of Technology is a common Unix-based window system. In addition to this GUI, a consortium of computer companies has produced the Common Desktop Environment (CDE) that is now very popular. Unix GUIs are discussed in Appendix B.

SUMMARY

This chapter presented an overview of computer philosophy and technology. Computers are tools that assist people in a multitude of tasks. Users should still check their work in fear of GIGO—"garbage in, garbage out." Computers are essentially lifeless, inert chunks of circuits and chips until activated and "brought to life" by software. Software programs perform instructions usually entered by users. System software, or the operating system, (OS) controls the interaction between hardware and software. Our focus, Unix, is one such operating system. Unix has many advantages, such as multitasking, networking, and portability. Though Unix still has no true standard, one of the most prevalent versions, SVR4, is the standard for this text.

KEY TERMS

bit	file system	resident module
byte	graphical user interface (GUI)	shell
directory	hardware	software
directory tree	kernel	Unix
file	operating system (OS)	

2

Sample Unix Session

2.1 NOTATION

Understanding technical writing requires familiarity with the author's notation. Unix commands and user input are styled in **boldface courier font**. ***Boldface italic courier*** font indicates that a name or value unique to your Unix session is called for: for instance, "***filename***" requires you to enter the name of a file that you have created—do *not* literally type "**filename**"! Output and all other Unix-related information you might see on a monitor are presented in `plain courier font`. Commentary on various commands is provided for you to study, and looks like this: *I am a comment; do not type me!* At various points, you will also be instructed to press certain keys such as the **Return** key. Many commands use the **Control** key. These special keystrokes are discussed in Section 2.2. Be sure to review this notation as summarized in Table 2-1.

2.2 CHARACTERS AND KEYBOARDS

Remember, GIGO (in case not, "garbage in, garbage out!"). You must be accurate on how you instruct Unix. Keyboarding is an important skill for all computer use.

2.2.1 ASCII Characters

As discussed in Chapter 1, computer data is stored as bits, a sequence of 1's and 0's. Because people prefer actual characters, the American Standard Code for Information Interchange (***ASCII***) was created. ASCII assigns 7-bit codes for 128 standard "characters" representing standard text such as letters, digits, and symbols, as well as special functions like *delete* and *backspace*. All 128 ASCII characters constitute the alphabet from which commands are created.

OBJECTIVES

After reading this chapter, you should be able to:

- Understand the computing environment in which you will practice
- Know important notation employed throughout the text
- Practice your first Unix session by logging on and off your computer network
- Experiment with a few Unix commands to develop a "feel" for Unix
- Respect important responsibilities and concerns of computer use

TABLE 2-1 Summary of Notation

NOTATION	MEANING
term	Key term in this text
`command`	Literal Unix command input—type this verbatim
`value`	General Unix input—type the name or value called for by this input
`^K`	Control+character—hold **Control** and hit the key called for (in the text, the circumflex, or caret, [^] is employed as a shorthand for the control key—don't hit the caret!)
`output`	Results of a Unix command or general Unix information
comment	Commentary on Unix command or output
Key	A particular key on the keyboard

APPLICATION: HOW TO READ AND USE COMPUTER TEXTBOOKS AND MANUALS

Without a doubt, some of the most boring reading comes not just from computer manuals, but *any* manuals. Have you ever tried reading recipes for fun? Frustration often results from the slow pace of memorizing any commands and syntax. To ease the learning process and alleviate the stress, follow these steps:

- *Familiarize yourself with the book*: Successful professionals don't know everything. They just know where to look. With any book you should first review the table of contents and quickly flip though all chapters and appendices. What information has the author provided to help you learn?

- *Review the book's organization*: Consider the table of contents as your guide to learning. Each section and subsection represents the portion of knowledge you must obtain and retain. Sorting out important material ahead of time will also help save time. Review suggestions typically provided in a preface or author's foreword.

- *Learn the notation*: All manuals and technical material employ notation, special styling (fonts, for example) that alert you to particular items, such as the computer commands in this text. Thoroughly understand all notation!

Otherwise, you might become confused and get stuck.

- *Set goals*: If you are taking a class, carefully read your assignment: knowing your "learning goals" will improve your motivation to slug through boring reading. If the goals seem unclear, review the beginning of the assigned section of the text. Never try to learn everything at once! Follow the author's suggested course outline or, perhaps, attempt one section at a time.

- *Practice reading*: Learning comes from both understanding *and* practice. Study the text *and* practice the commands! Having first reviewed the notation, skim a portion of the text a few times. Periodically remind yourself of chapter objectives. Knowing what happens and why it happens will help you retain the material.

- *Practice implementing*: Attempting and practicing commands eases memorization. Follow the suggested commands and exercises in the book. Understand *why* you are trying a command. Also, guess ahead of time the possible result. Read the text above and below each command for explanations of syntax and behavior. Further tips on practicing are presented in Chapter 3.

2.2.2 Standard Characters and Keys

Not all keyboards arrange characters the same way, but most have essentially similar features, as shown in Figure 2.1. Keys, or buttons you press, each activate input for the CPU to process. Names of all characters are categorized in Table 2-2 and summarized in Appendix A.

TABLE 2-2 Typical Keyboard Keys

CHARACTERS	DESCRIPTION
Lowercase English letters	**abcdefghijklmnopqrstuvwxyz** Press key with the appropriate letter.
Uppercase English letters	**ABCDEFGHIJKLMNOPQRSTUVWXYZ** Hold down Shift and the key with the appropriate letter.
Digits	**1234567890** Be careful not to type the letter O ("oh") instead of the number 0 (zero). Also, do not confuse the number one (1), for lowercase letter L (l).
Symbols	**!"#$%&'()*+,-./:;<=>?@[\]^_`{l}~ " "** In addition to these, a blank space is created by pressing the space-bar, the long bar at the bottom of the keyboard.
Special keys	**Esc**, **Tab**, **Control**, **Shift**, **Caps Lock**, **Alt**, **Meta (♦)**, **Backspace**, **Return**, **Enter** **"Alt"** and **"Meta"** are sometimes interchanged on keyboards. These keys are often used as keyboard shortcuts for menu-driven options.
Function keys	**F1**, **F2**, **F3**, **F4**, etc. These keys are typically assigned to various commands or functions for operating systems and particular software.
Arrow keys	→, ←, ↓, ↑ These keys move the cursor.
Miscellaneous	**Delete**, **Copy**, **Paste**, **Insert**, **Cut**, **Home**, **End**, **Page Up**, **Page Down**, **Num Lock**, etc. These keys often have unique uses specific to software packages, such as editors and word processors.

Figure 2.1. Example Keyboard

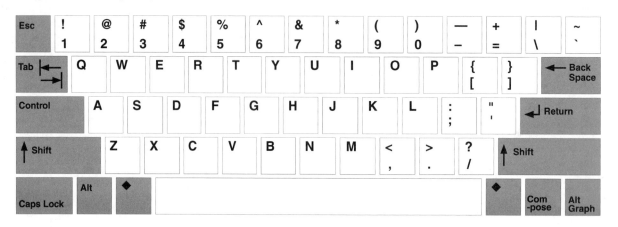

2.2.3 Special Keystrokes

Many commands employ *control characters*. The "beep," or bell sound that the computer can make, is signified as **^G**, and provides a common example. Activate **^G** by holding down **Control** and simultaneously pressing the **G** key. Do not actually type the caret (^)! In general, you can enter either **^g** or **^G**, but beware of case-sensitive application software.

PRACTICE!

> 1. What are two names for the character "^"?
> 2. What are two names for the character "-"?

2.3 SAMPLE SESSION

Now, it's time for your first Unix session. You will log in, play around, and then, log out. Of course, the "playing around" portion requires some work.

2.3.1 Obtain a Computer Account

Your site should supply you with an *account*, which provides space and privileges for using the site's computer system. Make sure that you learn how to access your account, too, because access methods do differ from system to system. A unique *username* identifies your account. The username, also referred to as *login name, user account,* or *user ID* is typically chosen by site administrators and abstracted from your real name. Throughout this text, I use my initials `dis` for my system's user ID.

2.3.2 Logging In

Locate a Unix computer site. Do not worry about remote access yet, because while it's convenient, your first session should take place where you can seek help. You commence a session when you log in, or, as some say, log on. Log in by typing your username at the `login` prompt. Next, press **Return** or **Enter**:

STEP 1: LOGIN | `login:` **dis** *Do Not Type "`login:`"! Press **Return** or **Enter** when finished typing.*

Did you make a mistake while typing? If so, press either **Backspace** or **Delete** to erase your mistake. If neither key works, try **^H**, the control sequence for backspace.

Now, the system will ask for your *password*, a special combination of characters, numbers, and symbols you create to protect your account. No one else should know your password! New users prompted to create a password should read Section 2.5 before continuing:

STEP 2: ENTERING YOUR PASSWORD | `Password:` *Type your password, then press **Return** or **Enter**.*

You will not actually see the characters as you type them—after all, the password is supposed to be secret, and maybe that person sitting near you is peeking. The computer system might "hang" for a moment while checking your account. Next, you might receive a welcome message or, alternately, be prompted to create a different password (see Section 2.5.). If you get the error message `incorrect password`, your login attempt failed. Try logging in and out again: perhaps you typed something wrong. Beware of **Shift** and **Caps Lock.** Unix is case-sensitive! Beware whether you enter upper- or lowercase letters.

2.3.3 Command Prompts

Assuming that you succeeded in logging in, Unix awaits your instructions. At this point, some new users erroneously think, "I've logged *in* to Unix," but that is not the case. In reality, you've logged *on* to your computer network using Unix. Recall from Chapter 1 that you are running a shell, a program that will interpret your instructions for Unix.

The shell prompts you for command entry. SVR4 comes with three main shells, each with different default prompts. The Bourne and Korn Shells use the dollar sign, ($), while the C Shell uses the percent symbol (%). Your system might even be customized with an entirely different prompt. Sometimes the prompt provides a date or computer name, such as (4:00pm)dis@mobius ~>. (Throughout this book, I will use an "ego" prompt, dis%, based on my username. Now, read and heed this warning: do not type the prompt!

2.3.4 Cursor

Cursors, such as █ or _, indicate where to type commands. With GUIs, your cursor might appear hollow (☐) and not accept input when the mouse is pointed outside the active window. To enable text entry, just point and click inside the desired window. For clarity, the cursor is usually not shown in examples throughout this text.

2.3.5 Command-Line Notation

You instruct a computer with ***commands***. In Unix, commands activate the shell to perform various tasks. Look at the sample command input and output in Figure 2.2: Everything that follows the prompt (dis%) composes the ***command line***—your input to Unix. The command line input terminates when you press **Return** or **Enter**. When you do that, Unix processes your instructions, then reports the results of its actions as output. If you make a mistake, Unix will usually respond with an error message.

Figure 2.2.   Sample Command Line Input and Output

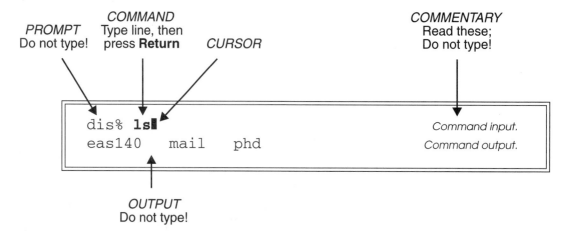

2.3.6 Command-Line Syntax

Unix has some general rules that you should heed:

- *Unix is case-sensitive:* It matters whether you use upper- or lowercase letters. Thus, for example, never type the command **ls** as "**Ls**," "**lS**," or even "**LS**."
- *Spaces:* Enter spaces with the spacebar. For example, to enter **ls ~dis**, do not type **ls~dis**. Instead, type **ls**, hit the spacebar, then type **~dis**. See the difference?
- *Dashes and underscores:* The underline, or underscore, symbol (_), is *not* the same as the dash, (–), or a blank space.

2.3.7 Entering Commands

Pretend that you have a momentary identity crisis. Try a simple command line, **who am i,** to find out your username:

STEP 3:
EXAMPLE
COMMAND LINE

```
dis% who am i
```
Be sure to type the command line with spaces in between each word

```
dis pts/0 Jul 8 19:42
```
Unix reports your username (pts), terminal ID (0), and login date and time (July 8, 7:42 P.M.).

This input **who am i** has two distinct components. The main Unix command is **who**, which, in general, reports everyone logged on to your system. The ***command options***, **am i**, modify the behavior of **who**, restricting its report to your identity only. Most commands have options, as demonstrated throughout this text.

PRACTICE!

> **3.** Is **am i** a valid Unix command line? Try entering **am i** to find out.
> **4.** What output does the command line **WHO AM I** provide?

2.3.8 What's My Shell?

Out of curiosity, determine your shell. Show SHELL, an environment variable, with the command **echo $SHELL**, and remember that Unix is case-sensitive! Entering **echo $*variable*** displays the value of ***variable***:

STEP 4:
SHOW DEFAULT
SHELL

```
dis% echo $SHELL
```
Report as output the value of SHELL. The dollar sign ($) indicates that the following item is a value.

```
/usr/local/bin/csh
```
Unix here reports a C Shell called "csh." Your actual shell might be different.

Unix sets SHELL and other environment variables each time you log on. These variables customize your Unix session and provide values for other commands and programs. (Consult Chapters 7 and 8 for more information.)

PRACTICE!

> **5.** What is your default system shell?
> **6.** Try the command line **echo SHELL.** What happens?

2.3.9 Logging Out

When you finish your work, you must end your session. You must remember to log out, or, as sometimes said, log off. Use the command **exit** to log out:

**STEP 5:
LOGOUT**

dis% **exit**   *Leave the system and terminate your session. If using a GUI, select a menu option to exit the entire session!*

login: *The login prompt should reappear.*

With C Shells, the command **logout** will end your session. Note that with a GUI, logging out of a single window usually does not fully end your session: typically, you must choose a menu option such as exit, log out, or Kill TWM. But, whether using a GUI or not, wait until you see the same screen or message from *before* you logged on, the login prompt. Only when that prompt reappears is your session over.

PRACTICE!

7. End your computer session, if you have not done so already.
8. Log in again.
9. Try logging out with the command **logout.** If the command fails, log off with **exit.** Why might the command have failed?

2.4 GENERAL ADVICE

This section addresses some Unix problems encountered by new and inexperienced users alike. If you get stuck anywhere along the way, refer back to this section.

2.4.1 Common Typing Mistakes

Sooner or later, you will make a typing error or typo. A misplaced or incorrect character can often cause bizarre results. Log in again, and deliberately enter this mistake:

**STEP 6:
MAKING
MISTAKES**

dis% **whoam i**   *With the space between the words deleted, the command becomes "**whoam**" rather than "**who am.**" There is no such command. This input is a deliberate mistake.*

whoam: Command not found.   *Unix reports your error.*

Congratulations! You have encountered one of your first Unix error messages. To avoid more, check for mistakes before hitting **Return** and entering the command. Use the **Backspace** or **Delete** keys to correct the typos. You can also usually move the cursor with the left- and right-arrow keys.

2.4.2 Something's Wrong?

Other things go wrong besides typing errors. Computers sometimes crash for their own reasons: too many users, too many processes, a software glitch, and system "hiccups" can all cause network-wide grief. Also, beware that not all versions of Unix produce the same results, so what suits one system may not work on another. You should consult a local-user guide specific to your system when studying this text to help avoid incompatibilities.

Most problems, though, are user related. Typing "bad" command lines, for instance, can often "freeze" or "hang" the computer. If this happens, always try pressing **^C**, the "kill" control sequence. Should that not help, try **^Z** as a last-ditch attempt to suspend your command. Out of courtesy, avoid suspending processes: suspended processes linger, and thus consume valuable CPU. Freezing and other common problems are diagnosed in Table 2-3.

2.4.3 Security

Always remember to log out! Never remain logged on if you leave your computer. Unscrupulous users could conceivably wreak havoc in your account and, perhaps, your life.

Even when you log off, do not turn off your computer. Typically, Unix terminals are left continuously running to avoid damaging the CPU. Booting a Unix computer can

TABLE 2-3 Unix Troubleshooting

PROBLEM	SOLUTION
The screen is blank before logging on.	• Press an inert key (**Shift,** for example) or jiggle the mouse.
Someone else is already logged on, or **who am i** reports the wrong user.	• Double check your assigned username. • Look around—maybe that person stepped away and did not log out. • Write down the username and log the person out. Then, log in and e-mail a reminder about the dangers of leaving an unattended computer.
After logging in, the computer accepts your username but then immediately logs you out.	• See a system administrator—you might be exceeding your disk quota.
After logging in, you get a message reading "Login incorrect."	• Do you have a valid account? • Did you enter the right username and password? • Did you choose the correct case while typing?
After logging in, the computer "hangs"—that is, no output is reported for a long time"	• Don't be impatient—sometimes the computer takes awhile to log you on.
You type a command and nothing happens.	• Did you press **Return** after typing?
During your session, the computer hangs.	• Too many users can slow a system. Be patient.
You type or press keys, but nothing appears on the screen.	• Did the system hang? Wait a few moments. • Did you accidentally press **^S**? This control sequence suppresses the output. To make the output visible again, press **^Q**. • Are you using a GUI? If so, try pointing your mouse inside the terminal window where you intend to type.
All your commands appear in UPPERCASE.	• Press the **Caps Lock** key. Now, try typing again.
You typed the wrong command and Unix is taking exceedingly long to perform this instruction.	• Wait and see what happens. You might learn something. • Kill the process with **^C**. • If **^C** does not work, suspend the process with **^Z**. • Sometimes **^D**, "exit," can help. But beware! **^D** might log you out. • If you are using a GUI, try destroying the window that contains the offending program.
The screen just went completely blank!	• Press **Shift** or an arrow key. Also, try jiggling the mouse. Monitors turn the picture off to prevent burning the image onto the screen.
It's an emergency, or you're completely stuck—and worse yet, there are no consultants to be found.	• Turn the computer off and on. Wait to see if you get logged out. Always save this option as a *last* resort! • Bug that person sitting next to you: claim total ignorance. You never know—one day that person might be *you* helping out another confused user.

be a lengthy process. Preferably, just leave idle or disabled computers alone. In an emergency, you might be able to find the on/off switch. However, you might then have to face an angry system administrator. Note that the monitors automatically shut off to conserve energy and prevent burning the login message onto the screen.

2.5 PROTECTING YOURSELF AND YOUR ACCOUNT

Respect general considerations and responsibilities inherent in using any networked computer. But, even if you independently own and operate a computer, abide by general rules of etiquette and national laws.

2.5.1 General Computer Use and Responsibility

Each computer site, Unix or otherwise, follows its own rules. Consult with your site administrator(s) about local policies: Visit an example site policy like http://wings.buffalo.edu/computing/policies/use.html. For more rules, see also Chapter 4.

2.5.2 Protecting Your Account from Intruders

Beware of crackers, people who try to cause computer mayhem. Crackers have powerful programs that might figure out, or "crack," your password and access your account. Follow these tips to protect yourself:

- Never share your account or tell anyone your password.
- Your password should contain at least six characters, at least one of which should be a number. Unix often distinguishes between upper- and lowercase letters. Unix will often accept other symbols as well.
- Your password should not contain something obvious about yourself, such as your birthday or address.
- Your password should not contain common words or expressions. For instance, "FORWHOMTHEBELLTOLLS" would be a bad choice.
- Never use anagrams of your username for your password. For example, username "dalessio" cannot have the password "soladies."

Changing your password is performed with the **passwd** command:

STEP 7:	dis% **passwd**	*Change your password.*
CHANGING		
YOUR	passwd: Changing password for dis	*Unix reports what's happening.*
PASSWORD	Old password:	*Enter your old password. You will not see the output.*
	New password:	*Enter the new password.*
	Re-enter new password:	*Retype your new password.*
	dis%	*If Unix accepts your new password, the prompt reappears.*

If Unix does not accept your new password, Unix reports an error message. Try changing the password again. Don't take it personally! Sometimes it takes a few tries. Password programs are often restrictive to maintain security. Also, the change is not always instantaneous. If you ever forget your password, visit your system administrator.

2.5.3 Warning: Carpal Tunnel Syndrome

Dangers accompany everything in life, computer use included. In fact, one facet of industrial-engineering studies ergonomics, how the human body interacts with the workplace environment. The human body is just not designed to sit still for many hours on end. Improper posture, poor typing practices, and extensive hours can physically harm your fingers, wrists, arms, and back. Conditions such as **carpal tunnel syndrome** (**CTS**) often result from excessive typing with poor posture. CTS can cause numbness, tingling, and pain in your hands and wrists. Check with your system administrator for handouts and guides for proper typing procedures, and consult the bibliography and Appendix E for suggested references on CTS.

SUMMARY

In this chapter, the basics of computing with Unix were introduced, beginning with the Unix "alphabet," the collection of symbols used to create Unix commands. The concept of commands was demonstrated in a sample session. After logging on, you experimented with a few Unix commands. Entering commands occurs at a prompt. The sequence of commands and other statements entered at the prompt is called a command line. Finally, your session ended with your logging out. Issues of responsible account use and safety concerns were also addressed.

KEY TERMS

ASCII	command line	control character
account	command option	password
carpal tunnel syndrome	command	username

Problems

1. If you have not done so already, obtain a Unix account.
2. Obtain site documents about policies, user accounts, and logging in. If your site provides Unix reference manuals, obtain those as well.
3. Where is consulting or Unix advice available at your computing site?
4. What are two names for the ASCII character "/"?
5. What is the difference between *logging on* and *logging in?*
6. What is the difference between *logging on* and *logging off?*
7. Log on and change your password.
8. What default shell is used by your Unix system?
9. Which version or type of Unix does your system use?
10. Does your system understand the BSD command **whoami**? What is one way of checking? Does the command work?
11. Suppose that someone entered the command line **ECHO $SHELL**, and Unix reported "ECHO: Command not found." What mistake did this person likely make? How should the command line have been typed?
12. Do you think that the password "chester" would be acceptable? Why or why not?
13. Name at least five items that you should consider when creating a password.
14. Who should know your password?
15. Consult your site's policies on responsible account usage. Name at least three guidelines.
16. What is CTS? Why should you be concerned? Does your site provide reference material on CTS?

3

File Editing

3.1 FILES

Engineers and scientists must manage all kinds of information. Conducting experiments, analyzing devices, designing systems, testing software, performing economic studies, and writing reports all generate heaps of data. This section introduces principles of managing data on a computer.

3.1.1 File Management

Files are collections of data, or documents that include reports, drawings, and papers, as discussed in Chapter 1. Data such as numbers, characters, pictures, and drawings constitute typical information. Think of files as just places for your "stuff."

Computers have eased the labor involved in storing such information by using *file management* programs. File management involves copying and moving files into directories that contain related information. Recall from Chapter 1 the directory tree shown in Figure 1.4 to picture how directories and files are organized. In this chapter, you will create your first files. Directories are reviewed in Chapter 5, while managing files is the subject of Chapter 6.

3.1.2 File Types

Many of the files that you will encounter and use are ASCII *text files*, composed of printable and viewable ASCII characters. ASCII includes lower- and uppercase letters, symbols, and digits shown in Table 2-2. Other ASCII characters perform actions like "new-line" (NL) and "null" (NUL). Other files, such as binary files, are composed of byte sequences that only the computer can read. Some examples of binary files include many Unix utilities, proprietary formats for application software, and archived files. (Refer to Chapter 7 for more information on binary files.)

OBJECTIVES

After reading this chapter, you should be able to:

- Understand the basics of ASCII text and file-naming conventions
- Learn and practice basic text-file editing with **vi**
- View text files with **more**
- List files in your account with **ls**
- Employ some commands related to producing hardcopy: **lp**, **lpstat**, and **cancel**

APPLICATION: HOW TO LEARN ABOUT COMPUTERS

Although elementary and high schools now commonly have their own computer labs, many students still suffer from computer phobias. Moreover, some feel ashamed or embarrassed about their lack of skill. I have often been vehemently told by a variety of students, young and old, that "computers *hate* me!"

Let me dispel this myth: Computers do *not* hate, let alone *feel* anything. Though we anthropomorphize computers, they are lifeless. Computers certainly never hold any particular grudges. Crackers might indeed have scores to settle, but *computers* do not. Moreover, I have witnessed students trembling in fear, worried that the next key they press will cause a horrible explosion or other tragic event. Granted, banging a table in anger toward a bug-ridden program *does* carry certain risks to CPUs (yes, I am guilty!). But, you have little chance of causing damage when simply typing commands. The wrong sequence of commands might mess up *your* account, and responsible studying can help prevent possible damage from that.

Experimentation is crucial with computers. Learn software according to this approach: locate and start the program, learn command syntax, solve problems, and demonstrate your work. Often, your system administrator, office, or school has supplied review sheets on activating programs—find them! They will help, but won't lessen your need to practice, *practice*, and ***practice***. Bring this book along with you to a computer. Read each section, try the commands. Look inside the book. Then, look up at your screen. Compare the two. Do you see what you expected to see? Read each portion of text during and after the command entry. Before entering a command, try to anticipate output.

At first, you might feel frustrated and incompetent, but these feelings do not indicate any lack of intelligence. Consider these feelings a challenge: becoming fed up with learning is the sign that you care to learn! After all, if you didn't care about learning, why would you feel anything at all? With practice, the commands will eventually sink in. Be sure to seek help if you get stuck. And have faith that one day all of these commands will seem like second nature—because they *will*.

3.1.3 ASCII Text Files

Although using ASCII limits presentation quality, ASCII text files are universal: You can transport your work among different computers throughout the world. Moreover, other formatting programs, such as TeX and PostScript, employ ASCII text commands to produce fonts, figures, and tables by using only text input. Other common uses of text files include electronic mail (e-mail), programming, and data files.

3.1.4 File Sizes

Each ASCII character contributes one byte to the file size. File size indicates the total memory consumed by a file's contents. Larger chunks, such as kilobytes and megabytes (see Table 1-1), usually help measure file sizes.

3.1.5 Filenames

Filenames are unique names assigned to files in order to help organize and identify your work. A Unix filename can include upwards of 255 characters and is normally restricted to ASCII characters. Unix prohibits only the slash (/) and NUL ASCII characters, but, you should generally choose from only letters, digits, the dot (.), and the underscore (_) to make filenames. Also, remember that Unix is case sensitive!

File extensions help identify the format of a file contents. They typically start with a dot (.) and usually abbreviate the file type with short text strings. For instance, basic text files often have the extension ".txt", and files in PostScript format are given the extension ".ps". Extensions, though, are more for convenience and often not required.

Some examples of filenames include `my_file.txt`, `Homework1`, and `12_16_ data_set.save`. Beware of using spaces in filenames (for example, "`bad file name.txt`"), because filenames with spaces and other strange characters are difficult to manage.

PRACTICE!

1. In kilobytes, calculate the size of a file containing 1024 ASCII characters.
2. Determine how many bytes are contained in the following sentence:
   `Unix is our friend!`
3. Suppose that you store a project in a file called `project#1_b.txt`. Did you choose an acceptable filename? Why or why not?

3.2 EDITING: CREATING AND SAVING TEXT FILES

A text editor can create, change, and view the contents of a text file. Modern, full-screen editors have antiquated older line-by-line editors, but *editing* a file still consists of four basic steps:

- *Starting* the editing program
- *Moving* the cursor
- *Inserting* and/or *deleting* text
- *Saving* or *destroying* your work

Whether you create a new file or change an older file, you still edit that file!

3.2.1 The **vi** Text Editor

The **vi** text editor is a standard Unix program. "**vi**" stands for *visual editor* and is pronounced *vee-eye*. Other editing programs, such as **pico** and **emacs**, are recommended if available. More experienced Unix users are encouraged to learn **emacs**, a powerful program with many features that extend beyond text editing. (Refer to Appendix C for basic descriptions and commands of **pica** and **emacs**.)

3.2.2 Creating Text Files with **vi**

Create a text file using **vi.** First, start the editor by entering the command **vi**:

STEP 8: START vi

    dis% vi   *Start the **vi** text editor. Do not forget to press **Return**.*

You can also enter **vi *filename*** to edit ***filename*** directly.

3.2.3 Command Mode

A column of tildes (~) spanning the entire height of the window or screen should appear on your monitor or window. The **vi** editor starts in ***command mode***, one of three **vi** modes:

STEP 9: vi START-UP SCREEN

    ▮   *vi starts in command mode (see below).*
    ~
    ~
    ~
    ~
    ~
    ~

While inside command mode, you can move the cursor around, delete and paste text, and toggle into other modes. To return to command mode from other modes, press the Escape key, **Esc**, just once. If you make a mistake, get incongruous results, or become confused, return to this mode.

3.2.4 Input Mode

Input mode lets you insert text into the file that you are editing. Type **i** at the prompt from within command mode to toggle into input mode. You can now enter text at the cursor. Press **Return** to finish one line and start the next:

STEP 10:
ENTERING TEXT

Type **i** *at the prompt to enter input mode! Do not press* **Return** *after typing* **i**.

Name: David I. Schwartz   *Enter this line, but type your own name! Press* **Return** *when done.*

To correct mistakes, move backwards with **Backspace**. *Then, type new characters directly over old characters at the cursor. Do not use the arrow keys!*

Username: dis   *Enter this line, but use your own username! Press* **Return** *when done.*

If you need to delete a line, press **Esc** *to enter command mode. Next, move up or down with the arrow keys ↑ and ↓. Then, type* **dd** *to delete the offending line. Go back to input mode by typing* **i**.

█   *The cursor marks the current position of text entry.*

~   *A column of tildes (~) appears on the remaining portion of the monitor or window.*
~
~

Beware that **vi** is case-sensitive! For instance, entering **I** instead of **i** inserts text at the beginning of a line as opposed to the current cursor position.

3.2.5 Last-Line Mode

"Saving your work" means telling **vi** to preserve your file contents inside your account. To save your work, you must switch to *last-line mode*. Last-line mode lets you save and quit, as well as set **vi** options, search for text, and name or rename files. Right now, though, follow these steps to save your work.

Enter last-line mode by typing a colon (:) from within command mode. Then, enter **wq *filename*** to save your text as ***filename*** inside your account:

STEP 11:
SAVING YOUR
WORK

Press **Esc** *to reestablish command mode.*

Type a colon (:) The bottom line of your screen or window will show the colon. You are now in last-line mode.

Name: David I. Schwartz   *Previously typed text.*
Username: dis   *Previously typed text.*

~
~
~

:wq info.txt   *Type a colon to enter last-line mode*
Save your work to file called info.txt.   *In this sequence, type* **wq**, *Spacebar,* **info.txt**, *and* **Return**.

"info.txt" [New File] 2 lines, 54 characters   **vi** *reports your filename.*
dis%   *You just left* **vi**. *Your Unix prompt reappears.*

The **w** commands instructs Unix to write all text into a file, whereas **q** tells Unix to quit **vi**.

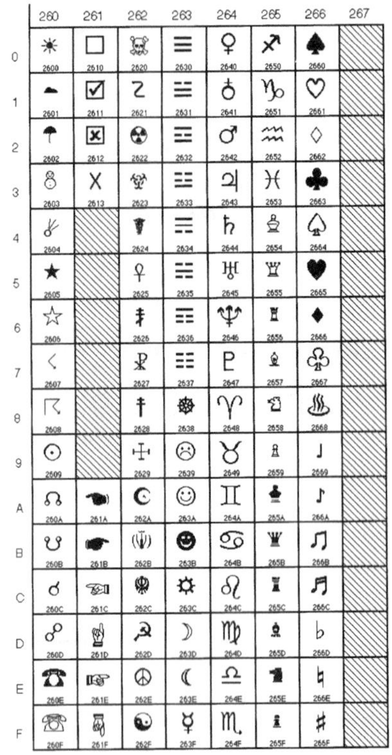

Figure 3.1. Code chart of miscellaneous symbols, U+2600–267F. Reproduced with permission of Unicode, Inc.

PRACTICE!

4. Create a text file `test.txt` by entering **vi *filename***.
5. What does the bottom of the screen or window say? What is your current mode?
6. Enter these sentences on two separate lines using **vi**
   ```
   This is a test of vi.
   Do not panic. vi is just a text editor!
   ```
7. Enter command mode and select last-line mode. Why should you now enter **wq**?

3.3 EDITING: CHANGING TEXT FILES

Remember that editing involves more than simply creating and saving files. Editing includes viewing and changing file contents as well. This section introduces **vi** commands that enable more efficient file editing.

3.3.1 Additional **vi** Commands

Skim over the basic **vi** command listing shown in Table 3-1. Note that most of these commands are entered from the command mode. When working inside *input mode*, only the **Return**, **Del**, **Backspace**, and **Tab** keys can move the cursor.

3.3.2 Changing Text Files

Editing also involves changing file contents. Enter **vi *filename*** to edit your file `info.txt`. **vi** will create ***filename*** if ***filename*** does not exist. Practice editing by removing the text "`Name:`" and "`Username:`".

**STEP 12:
EDITING TEXT
FILES**

Remember that **vi** *commences in command mode!*   *Press* **Esc** *whenever you need this mode.*
```
David I. Schwartz
```
*Delete "*Name:*": Type* **x** *when the cursor is over each character.*
Type **l** *or* **h** *to move the cursor right or left.*

Move the cursor to the next line.   *Press* **Esc** *for command mode. Next, type* **j** *or the
down arrow key (↓).*

```
dis
```
*Delete "*Name:*": position the cursor on each character and type* **x**.

Add a line below the current line.   *Type* **o** *to switch to insert mode and create a new line.*
blue   *Enter your favorite color.*

```
~
```

```
~
```

Enter command mode, and then, last-line mode.   *Press* **Esc***, and then, colon (***:***).*
```
:wq
```
Save your work and quit **vi**.

```
"info.txt" 3 lines, 27 characters
```
All work is saved in the current file info.txt.

```
dis%
```
You just left **vi**. *Your Unix prompt reappears.*

TABLE 3-1 Common **vi** Commands

CURSOR MOVEMENT		INSERTING TEXT	
One character right	**l** or →	Append at end of line	**A**
One character left	**h** or ←	Append to right of cursor	**a**
One line down	**j** or ↓	Insert at beginning of line	**I**
One line up	**k** or ↑	Insert to left of cursor	**i**
End of line	**$**	Open new line above current line	**O**
Beginning of line	**0**	Open new line below current line	**o**
Cutting/Pasting		Deleting Text	
Copy ("yank") line into memory	**yy** or **Y**	Delete current character	**x**
Copy to end of line	**y$**	Delete to end of line	**d$**
Paste line after or below cursor	**P**	Delete to beginning of line	**d0**
Paste line before or above cursor	**p**	Delete current line	**dd**
Saving Work		Quitting **vi**	
Save work to current file	**:w**	Quit; ignore any changes	**:q!**
Save work to file	**:w file**	Quit (assumes no changes)	**:q**
Save work to file and quit	**:wq file**	Save changes and quit	**:wq**
"Undo" Commands		Search File	
Undo previous command	**u**	Search forward for **text**	**/text**
Undo editing changes to line	**U**	Search backward for **text**	**?text**

3.3.3 Basic **vi** Editing Steps

In general, follow this pattern when editing with **vi**:

- **vi** starts from command mode, in which you can move the cursor around and delete offending text. Change your mode when you finishing moving and deleting.
- Next, toggle to input mode. Use **a**, **A**, **i**, **I**, **o**, or **O** to insert text on one line. Press **Return** for a new line, or press **Esc** to return to command mode. Repeat this cycle until you finish editing.
- Finally, press **:** to initiate last-line mode. Save your work and exit with **wq**.

Relations between these three modes are summarized in Figure 3.2. **vi** can be confusing, so frequently consult this diagram as you switch among modes.

Beware that your text files might not properly print if you type excessively long lines. From within last-line mode, enter **set wrapmargin=1** to ensure text wraps around. See Problem 13 for more details.

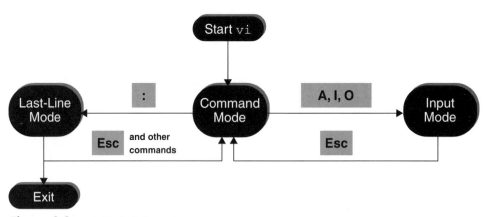

Figure 3.2. **vi** Mode Schematics

PRACTICE!

8. Load `info.txt` into **vi** again.
9. Insert the labels "`Name:`", "`Username:`", and "`Favorite Color:`" at the beginning of the appropriate lines.
10. Save your work and quit.

3.4 BASIC FILE COMMANDS

A multitude of Unix commands operate on files, but many GUI programs have rendered certain commands obsolete. Still, text-based commands can greatly assist routine file management. More commands are introduced in Chapters 5 and 6.

3.4.1 Basic File Listing

Your account reserves your personal space, a directory in which to store your own files and directories. Thankfully, remembering a potentially vast collection of "stuff," and where it resides, is unnecessary. When you log in, Unix starts inside **_HOME_**, the "top" directory for your account. To see what is in HOME, use the command **ls**, which calls up a listing of a directory's contents:

STEP 13: **LIST FILES**	`dis% `**`ls`**	*List files contained in HOME directory.*
	`info.txt test.txt`	*The two text files created in the Practice problems are listed.*

Additional files and directories might also be listed.

3.4.2 Viewing Files

To see a file's contents without editing it, use the **more** command. The command line **more *filename***, for example, displays the contents of ***filename*** on your screen:

STEP 14: VIEW **TEXT FILE**	`dis% `**`more info.txt`**	*View file* `info.txt`*.*
	`Name: David I. Schwartz`	*The file contents are displayed on your screen.*
	`Username: dis`	*I am assuming that you did the Practice problems in Section 3.3.*
	`Favorite Color: blue`	*This is the last line of the* `info.txt` *file.*
	`dis%`	*Now the command prompt follows the file contents.*

Unix will report "`No such file or directory`" if the requested file does not exist.

The command **more** is called a "pager," because with it you can step, or "page," through portions of a file at your own pace. Pressing Return moves the display one line forward, while pressing the Spacebar will leap ahead entire "pages," or screens. If you are looking for a particular word, try entering the word preceded by a slash (**/*word***). **more** will search for the next occurrence of ***word***: Typing **n** will find the next occurrence. If the viewing ever becomes garbled, try clearing the screen with **^L**. Should paging becomes tedious, type **q** to quit **more**.

PRACTICE!

> 11. Suppose that you wish to view a large text file, `big.txt`, that has several pages. Create a text file called `big.txt` using **vi**.
> 12. Go to input mode and enter at least 100 lines of anything. Try not to bang on **Return** too hard.
> 13. Exit **vi**. What are three commands that will confirm the existence of your `big.txt` file?
> 14. View `big.txt` with **more.** Try pressing both **Return** and the Spacebar. What is reported at the bottom of the screen until **more** finishes?

3.5 PRINTING FILES

Sooner or later, you will have to submit something for grading or review. Typically, engineers and scientists must print their work in the form of ***hardcopy***—file contents that are printed on paper. In fact, sometimes hardcopy is called a "printout."

The SVR4 print command is **lp**, which stands for "line printer," but a trick to remembering this command is to think of "laser printing," a common printing method. Some versions of Unix use an older BSD print command, **lpr**, rather than **lp**.

Use **lp info.txt** to print **info.txt** on your default system printer:

<table>
<tr><td>

STEP 15:
PRINT FILES

</td><td>

```
dis% lp info.txt
```

```
request id is ntx-1793 (1 file(s))
```

</td><td>

Print your info.txt *file. Be sure to have created it first!*

Unix reports the "name" of your printing process.

</td></tr>
</table>

Note Unix's response to the print command line. The request id line is composed of ***printer-number***. The number labels your ***print job***, which is your request to Unix to print a file. (Actually, processes that you activate in Unix are often called *jobs* as discussed in Chapter 7.) **lp** works by ***spooling*** a file. Spooling first involves informing Unix which file to print. Next, Unix instructs the printer on how to format the printout, that is, how the file looks on paper.

To learn your default system printer, try entering **echo $PRINTER** or **echo $LPDEST**. If you know names of other printers, use **lp -d *printer filename*** to specify one other than your default. Consult your computing site for listings of printer names. In this command line, **-d** is the destination command option for **lp**. Use **-d** to direct your output to a printer or print site different than the default. Note that the printer name must follow **-d**. The BSD syntax is **lpr -P *printer filename***.

You can monitor the status of your print job with **lpstat**:

<table>
<tr><td>

STEP 16:
CHECK PRINT-
JOB STATUS

</td><td>

```
dis% lpstat
```

```
ntx-1793   dis   163   Nov 22 18:30
```

</td><td>

What is the status of pending print jobs?

The print job is still pending.

</td></tr>
</table>

Unix usually reports the request ID, username, file size in bytes, and the date and time of the request. Pending print jobs might be waiting for other files to print, or perhaps, might be currently printing. If **lpstat** reports nothing at all, your request might have been processed faster than you could enter **lpstat**.

Sometimes you will change your mind about certain printouts. To cancel a print job, use **cancel *requestID*** as in, cancel **ntx-1796**. Unix will endeavor to remove the print job from the spool, assuming that the file has not already been printed:

<table>
<tr><td>

STEP 17:
CANCEL PRINT
JOB

</td><td>

```
dis% lp info.txt
```

```
request id is ntx-1796 (1 file(s))
```

Quickly enter the command below!
```
dis% cancel ntx-1796
```

```
request "ntx-1796" cancelled
```

</td><td>

Print info.txt *again. Unix will now inform you when done.*

Note the request ID.

lpstat *will also give the request ID.*
Cancel the print job with your own request ID.

The print job got cancelled.

</td></tr>
</table>

Investigate also the BSD versions for print-queue (**lpq**) and print-removal (**lprm**).

PRACTICE!

15. Create a new text file called `new.txt`.

16. Write a few lines of text inside `new.txt`.

17. Determine your default system printer.

18. Print `new.txt` on your default printer. Is another printer available? If so, print `new.txt` with that printer as well.

19. How do you determine when the print job finishes?

3.6 APPLICATION: PROGRAM EDITING

In this section, you will employ newly learned Unix skills to develop a program. Later chapters will use this program to demonstrate further applications of Unix.

3.6.1 Problem

Pretend that you are an engineer working for D.I.S., Inc., a consulting firm that develops software for clients. D.I.S. was recently hired to produce software that outputs `Hello World!`, and your boss assigned your department to this task. You, the lucky engineer, have the job of prototyping the software.

3.6.2 Background

A popular programming language is C++. Programs are typically written in ASCII text and compiled into byte-code. Unix provides many *compilers*, programs that create executable programs. A C++ compiler converts the C++ text into commands, software the computer can execute.

3.6.3 Methodology

Developing software involves a sequence of steps. First, you will write the program, and in later chapters, you will perform more tasks associated with the work. In this portion, you will:

- Define your task—develop software to report a message to the screen
- Edit a file—compose the code, and store it in an ASCII text file
- Check your work—view file contents and produce hardcopy for review

3.6.4 Solution

Use the filename `hello.C`, an appropriate-sounding name for the task at hand. Use **vi** to create the text file:

STEP 18: CREATE A PROGRAM

```
dis% vi hello.C
```
Create your program, `hello.C`, *written in C++.*

The following code includes a sequence of inert comments, functions, and commands—anything commencing with **//** is considered a comment and is ignored by compilers. Functions like **main(void)** perform tasks and return values when finished. "**main**" starts the program and is labelled "**int**" to return an integer when finished, whereas "**cout**" is a function for producing output. Lines such as "**#include**" tell the C++ compiler to load functions stored in system files like "**iostream.h**".

STEP 19:
HELLO WORLD
PROGRAM

```
// "hello.C"
// Created by <your name>
// This program prints "Hello World!"
// to the screen.

#include <iostream.h>
int main(void)
{
    cout << "HELLO WORLD!";

    return 0;
}

~

~

~

:wq
```

Enter the text exactly as you see.
Anything following // is considered commentary
and is ignored by the compiler.

"Include" files incorporate common functions.
*Your first function is called **main**.*
Begin a code segment with an open brace({).
Print the message, HELLO WORLD!
End each code line with a semicolon (;).
The program returns a value of zero when finished.
End the code segment with a closed brace (}).

*Empty lines inside the **vi** editor.*

When finished, enter last-mode. Now, save and quit.

Do not worry about C++ for now—later courses will demonstrate programming. Now that you have created and saved your program, check your work with Unix commands. You should also print hardcopy to document your work:

STEP 20:
CHECKING
WORK

```
dis% ls
```
List current files.

```
hello.C
```
You will probably see other files as well.

```
dis% more hello.C
```
View the contents of hello.C.

You will see the contents of hello.C. Check them against your assignment— do you see a mistake? Hint: Is it Hello or HELLO that the program should say?

```
dis% vi hello.C
```
Drat! You made a mistake! Your client wants Hello World!, not HELLO WORLD! Go back and edit the file.

```
dis% more hello.C
```
View the contents of hello.C.

You will see the contents of hello.C again. Did you fix the mistake?

```
dis% lp hello.C
```
*Print a copy of your program. Use **-d printer** to send the job to another printer.*

```
request id is ntx-1022 (1 file(s))
```

```
dis% lpstat
```
Check the status of your print job.

```
ntx-1022      dis      234     Oct 25 9:06
```
The print job is still pending.

In the next chapter, you will use e-mail to perform further tasks.

SUMMARY

The basics of the Unix file management were discussed. One common task is editing text files with programs such as **vi**. Editing consists of creating and changing files. There are three main modes in **vi**. Most commands are entered from within command mode, from which the user can move the cursor, delete text, or enter other modes. Text is entered using input mode. Saving and quitting are activated in last-line mode. Such text files can then be displayed, but not edited, with **more**. You can display the contents of a directory with **ls**. **lp** and **lpstat** are commands for producing printouts and managing print jobs.

KEY TERMS

editing	hardcopy	**vi** command mode
file extension	HOME	**vi** input mode
file management	print job	**vi** last-line mode
filename	spooling	
file	text file	

Problems

1. What is a computer file?
2. Name at least three uses for files.
3. How many standard ASCII characters are available for use in constructing text files?
4. How many ASCII characters are used in the following line;
   `Interval Addition: [1,2] + [3,4] = [4,6]`
5. What are three uses for a text editor?
6. How many bytes are in a file composed of three blank lines? Assume that this file was created by inserting three blank lines using **vi**.
7. Is the **vi** last-line-mode command "**:qw**" the same as "**:wq**?" Which command sequence is permissible?
8. Are the filenames HELLO.txt and hello.txt identical? Why or why not?
9. Is the command line **vi vi** valid if you are working inside your account?
10. If you start **vi** without a filename, how do you save your work to a file called save_this.txt from within **vi**?
11. Is the command **less** available on your system? If so, what does **less** do?
12. Try the commands **tail** and **head** on a large text file. What do these commands do?
13. Project 1: Create a text file called .exrc. Enter the following lines inside:
    set showmode
    set wrapmargin=1
    Why will this file ease your work? Find out by entering **man vi** at the Unix prompt.
14. Project 2: Create a text file called hw1.txt. Type in all problems and solutions for this chapter. Type your name at the top of the file. Print your work to hardcopy when finished.
15. Project 3: Create a text file called commands.txt. Describe in an organized and clear fashion how the Unix commands **cancel**, **exit**, **lp**, **ls**, and **more** function. Be sure to include syntax, usage, and an example. Type your name at the top of the file. Print your work when complete.
16. Project 4: Write a one- to three-page, double-spaced essay about why are you studying Unix. Somewhere in the essay, describe how and why you are interested in science or engineering. Do not be afraid to be candid. Edit your work *entirely* with a text editor. Be sure to manually check your grammar, spelling, and overall style. Also, try **spell *filename***. Enter your name at the top of the file. Print and submit your file when finished.

4

Communication and the Internet

4.1 COMMUNICATION

All projects require communication. Whether talking to coworkers, sending updates, or writing reports, human interaction is essential. Traditional means of communication include memos and telephones. Computers have enhanced such communications with data transfer, Web browsing, and e-mail. Unix provides a wide variety of utilities well suited to these tasks.

4.2 NETWORKING AND THE INTERNET

To communicate with one another, computers require a network. Networks of connected computers exist on local and global scales.

4.2.1 LAN

A *local area network* (**LAN**) connects a group of computers that are in relatively close proximity to one another. Each computer connected to the LAN "listens" for *packets*, small bursts of electronic data. **Protocols** govern how networked computers interact while transferring such information. Many protocols feature common programs, such as FTP and **telnet**, both of which are discussed in this chapter. Unix employs *transmission control protocols/internet protocols* (**TCP/IP**). Unfortunately, fully describing TCP/IP is beyond the scope of this text, but you should know that Unix shares these protocols with the Internet. In fact, one of Unix's greatest strengths is this "natural understanding" of the Internet.

4.2.2 The Internet

A *wide area network* (**WAN**) connects a geographically dispersed conglomeration of computers that share informa-

OBJECTIVES

After reading this chapter, you should be able to:

- Use Unix communication programs
- Understand concepts of local and global networking
- Understand Internet concepts such as domain names and protocol transfer methods
- Demonstrate local and global communication with e-mail, file transfer, and Web browsing

tion. The ***Internet*** is the largest of all WANs, with millions of nodes, or connected computers. The Internet evolved out of the ARPANET, a communications network devised by the United States military to survive a nuclear attack. Today, commercial, educational, and private organizations dominate the Internet which has rapidly become a necessity for research, information, commerce, advertising, and entertainment.

Who's in charge? Technically, no one controls the Internet. However, several organizations, such as the Internet Engineering Task Force (IETF), the Internet Architecture Board (IAB), and the Internet Society (ISOC) help set standards.

4.2.3 IP Addresses and Hostnames

Computers connected to the Internet have unique identifiers called ***IP addresses***, which take the form $n.n.n.n$, where n is a number between 0 and 255. Every IP address also has a ***hostname***. For instance, hostname "whitehouse.gov" has the IP address 198.137.241.30. Your system's "Welcome" message should indicate the system's hostname. Try **host *hostname*** to identify your hostname's IP address.

The hostname is a sequence of computer and network names. In this example, the name "whitehouse" is the host, the actual network connected to the Internet. This hostname has only one element, but many hostnames includes more elements that are separated by dots. Each of these elements correspond to local networks called *subnets* and *subdomains*. The final portion, "gov," is called a ***domain***, the most general classification of the host.

The five standard Internet domains denote the nature of the domain's classification: *com* (commercial), *edu* (educational), *gov* (government), *mil* (military), *net* (Internet-access providers), and *org* (nonprofit and private organizations). Other common domains include two-letter country abbreviations, such as "uk" for Great Britain and "jp" for Japan. The Internet Network Information Center (InterNIC) currently assigns domains and hostnames.

4.3 LOCAL COMMUNICATION

Daily computer work demands communication. Among other things, monitoring system changes, warnings, and upgrades helps maintain your account. You may also wish to communicate with classmates, instructors, coworkers, and friends who have accounts on your computer system.

4.3.1 Keeping Up to Date

Staying abreast of important information isn't too difficult. Learn to communicate with system administrators. You can rely on them to fix account problems and dispense advice. Take the time to check site announcements, which are usually posted on Web pages and in USENET. Always read the welcome message when you log in. Some systems also implement **news**, a command for relaying important system updates. Try entering **news -s** to produce a count of unread updates on your account:

STEP 21:
SYSTEM NEWS

```
dis% news -s
```
Report a count of all news items.

```
No news.
```
*... is good news! Enter **news** if a number is shown.*

Enter **news** with no options to read new messages or updates. Rather than **news,** some older systems might employ **motd**, *message of the day,* instead.

You can also use Unix to keep track of the time, date, and month:

Figure 4.1.   Bridge monitoring. Courtesy of Stuart S. Chen.

**STEP 22:
DISPLAY DATE
AND TIME**

```
dis% date

Tue Dec 16 11:59:59 EST 1997
```

Check the day, date, time, and year.

EST = Eastern Standard Time.

Figure 4.2.   Bridge monitoring. Courtesy of Stuart S. Chen.

4.3.2 Who's On-line?

Remember the identity-crisis command line, **who am i**? The command **who**, used alone, provides a list of everyone currently logged on to your network:

STEP 23:
CHECK WHO IS
LOGGED ON

```
dis% who                                    Who else is logged on?

[list of users]           You might even see yourself listed more than once, due to GUIs.
                                (Each window represents a separate connection.)
```

For determining users on remote systems, try **rusers**. For a list of all users who have system access, try **listusers**.

Another related command is **finger**. Like **who**, entering **finger** by itself will also show a list of people currently logged in. With options, **finger** will investigate a single person. Try **finger -m** *username*:

STEP 24:
FIND
INFORMATION
ABOUT
ANOTHER USER

```
dis% finger -m chz                          Check up on user chz.
```

Automatically display login name, HOME directory, last login, and e-mail status.

```
Login name: chz In real life:         Chester Zeshonski
Directory: /home/chz                       Shell: /bin/csh
Last login Fri Nov 27 13:31
New mail received Sat Nov 29 00:23:17 1997;
   unread since Fri Nov 28 17:00:23 1997
```

Display text stored in chz's finger plan file, if it exists.

```
Plan:
Avoid conformity/boredom as long as possible.
```

This output indicates that Chester used a *finger plan*, a file called .plan inside HOME created to respond to **finger** requests.

Use **finger -m** *username* only when you know *username*. If you are unsure, try **finger** *lastname*, or, if you are truly desperate, try **finger** *firstname*. Beware, though, that **finger** can act differently depending on a host system's security concerns. If you need further information, try Web services such as http://www.four11.com.

4.3.3 Talk with Others

The command **talk** enables you to write messages to another user currently on-line. If you both logged on to the same system, use **talk** *username*. For "long distance" chatting over different, but connected systems, use *username@hostname*. The **talk** command acts like a telephone: **talk** "rings" into a person's computer session by flashing on her or his monitor a message indicating your desire to "talk." The other person can respond with **talk** *yourusername.*

The following sequence will illustrate this procedure. Assume that someone named Craig with username crs is currently logged in. To "call" Craig, enter **talk crs**:

STEP 25:
WRITING
MESSAGES TO
ANOTHER USER

dis% **talk crs**   *Call Craig user* crs *to talk.*

For the sake of the exercise, assume that your username is dis. As a result of your **talk** command, Craig gets a message that dis wants to talk. To respond, Craig would enter **talk dis** if dis is on the same system. Craig could also enter **talk dis@mobius.eng.buffalo.edu** if dis logged on to a different system:

STEP 26:
RESPONDING
TO MESSAGES
TO ANOTHER
USER

crs *would see this message suddenly flash somewhere on his computer monitor:*

```
Message from Talk_Daemon@mobius.eng.buffalo.edu at 23:10 ...
talk: connection requested by dis@mobius.eng.buffalo.edu.
talk: respond with: talk dis@mobius.eng.buffalo.edu
```

crs% **talk dis**   crs *would enter this command to respond to* dis.

At this point your screen will split in half. Each person types in the top half, while the messages from the other person appear in the bottom half. Whether or not you initiate contact, you will always enter text in the top:

STEP 27:
SAMPLE TALK
SESSION

```
Hi Craig. What's up?                                   You always type up here.
------------------------------------------------------------
Not much. How's your Unix book going?       crs's message appears down here.
```

When the boxes become cluttered, clear the screen with **^L**. To exit **talk**, enter **^C**—but before you do, be courteous and warn your friend that you will soon quit.

Sometimes you will not want to talk. To block incoming calls, enter the command line **mesg n**. Entering **mesg y** will permit your account to accept messages again. Check your blocking status with **mesg**.

Another communication tool is **send**, assuming that your system supports the program. **send** has the advantage of sending e-mail if the person whom you are trying to reach is not logged on.

PRACTICE!

1. What does the **cal** command do? What day of the week is December 16, 2067?
2. Finger your own username. What information does Unix provide about you?

4.4 E-MAIL

Why are regular letters sent via the post office called "snail-mail"? Because electronic mail, or *e-mail*, arrives much quicker for less effort. E-mail messages are composed of electronic data sent to and collected by people on networked computers. This section provides an overview of Unix e-mail programs.

Figure 4.3. Bridge monitoring. Courtesy of Stuart S. Chen.

4.4.1 E-mail Addresses

To deliver your snail-mail, the postal service requires an address that specifies the person and place you wish to send your mail. With e-mail, you must do much the same, only with an ***e-mail address***, which typically is expressed as `username@hostname`. Many programs will automatically append the "`@hostname`" portion when the `username` is on a local system.

Figure 4.4. Bridge monitoring. Courtesy of Stuart S. Chen.

4.4.2 E-mail Programs

If you have received new e-mail since your last Unix session, your system will often report "You have mail" when you log on. Some GUI programs, such as **xbiff**, even sound a beep when mail arrives during a session. You receive mail in a unique mailbox assigned to your account, and specific files in the Unix directory tree store e-mail. These files are normally found in the directory paths /var/mail/*username* or /usr/ mail/*username*. (Consult Chapters 5 and 6 for more information on directories.) Rarely do you need to view these files, because e-mail programs allow you to access your mail through more convenient means.

Most Unix systems employ a variety of text-based e-mail programs, including **mail**, **mailx**, **pine**, and **elm**. GUIs like **xmail** and **dtmail** provide pull-down menu options. Netscape mail is even more advanced—with it, you can mail messages in different formats and fonts. SVR4 provides **mail** as well as **mailx**, a more advanced version of **mail**. If available, new users are encouraged to learn **elm** or **pine**. These are excellent text-based e-mail programs with simple user interfaces (see Appendix D).

4.4.3 E-mailing a Message

To mail a message, enter **mailx _username_**. (Not sure of the username? Try **finger**, as described in Section 4.3. Also, note that the command and program typically have identical names.) **mailx** usually prompts you for a Subject, a label that describes your message's contents. After typing a subject line (leaving the Subject blank is often considered rude) and pressing **Return**, you are in input mode. Begin typing your message, but be forewarned: in standard input mode, you cannot edit lines after pressing **Return**. When you are through typing, press **^D** at the beginning of a new line to transmit your message.

Try e-mailing a message to yourself:

STEP 28: **SEND E-MAIL**	dis% **mailx dis**	*Mail a message to yourself: Enter your own username where "dis" appears here.*
	Subject: **test1**	*This message just tests* **mailx**.
	This is test#1 of mailx.	*Press* **Return** *when you finish typing.*
	^D	*Enter* **^D** *on a new line to send the message.*
	EOT	*The message "end of text" (EOT) will appear when you finish composing the e-mail.*
	dis%	*Your Unix prompt reappears after the system sends the e-mail.*

Your message has now been sent to yourself. Had you chosen another person, the message would have been sent to that user. Remember, write with care! Once sent, e-mail cannot be recalled.

You can avoid making errors, though, by taking advantage of some of **mailx**'s advanced options, like the tilde escape commands. Entered as **~_command_**, these commands operate inside input mode and perform some handy tasks: **~r _filename_**, for example, will load a text file **_filename_** into the e-mail you are sending. You can enter **~v** to invoke **vi**, or the default visual editor so that you can edit messages before sending. The list of all **~** commands are found by entering **~?**.

<table>
<tr><td rowspan="10">

STEP 29:
EDIT AN
E-MAIL
MESSAGE
BEFORE
SENDING

</td><td>

```
dis% mailx dis
```
</td><td>*E-mail yourse*</td></tr>
</table>

STEP 29: **EDIT AN** **E-MAIL** **MESSAGE** **BEFORE** **SENDING**	`dis% ` **`mailx dis`**	*E-mail yourse.*
	`Subject: ` **`test2`**	*This will be your second .*
	`~v`	*Type ~v. Next, press **Return**. You are now in **vi**, or visual editor, mode.*
	`To: dis`	*Some systems will let you change message address information at this point.*
	`Subject: test2`	*You do not need to change these settings.*
	`This is test #2 of mailx.`	*Type **i**. Input your message using the text-editor commands.*
	`:wq`	*Press **Esc**. Assuming you are in **vi**, "save message and exit **vi**." You have not sent your message yet. You can enter more commands, continue writing, or send the e-mail with ^D.*
	`^D`	*Send e-mail.*
	`EOT`	*Your message has been transmitted.*
	`dis%`	*The Unix prompt reappears.*

4.4.4 Reading E-mail

Read new e-mail by entering the command **mailx** with no arguments. When you do, **mailx** first will indicate that you are in command mode by displaying the query (?) prompt. Each message is shown with a ***header*** (see Figure 4.5). Pressing **Return** will display the message marked with a >, whereas entering a message's number will cause that message to be displayed:

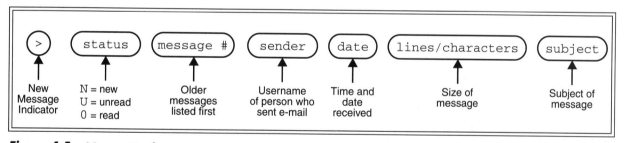

Figure 4.5. Message Headers in **mailx**

STEP 30: **READING** **E-MAIL**	`dis% ` **`mailx`**	*Read new mail.*
	`mailx version 5.0 [date] Type ? for help`	***mailx** reports version and date.*
	`"/var/mail/dis": 2 messages 2 unread`	***mailx** shows your system mail directory and message counts.*
	`>N 1 david i schwartz Wed Oct 26 00:03 16/667 test`	*The current message is marked with a ">."*
	`N 2 david i schwartz Wed Oct 26 00:13 16/657 test2`	*This the next message. "N" means that it's also unread.*

```
?
```
"?" is the command-mode prompt. Press **Return** *to read the message marked with "*>*." You can also type 2, then the* **Return** *key, to see the second message.*

```
?q
```
Enter **q** *to quit.*

The first time you use **mailx**, a file called mbox is created inside your HOME directory. Unless you specifically delete them, all read messages will be appended to mbox. Unread messages will remain unstored and be listed with status "U" when you run **mailx** again. More commands are listed in Table 4-1.

TABLE 4-1   **mailx** Command Mode Commands

COMMAND	DESCRIPTION
?	Show all commands and descriptions
h	List all current messages
s *filename*	Save message by appending to filename
d	Delete message
u	Undelete message
R *message*	Reply to sender of message (specify with number)
q	Quit **mailx;** remove read and deleted messages
x	Exit **mailx** without removing any messages

4.4.5 Responsibilities

Check with your system administrators about proper e-mail use. In general, treat your e-mail as you would regular snail-mail. Never:

- Forward e-mail without permission
- Make any threats, harass people, or say anything that is illegal
- Do anything else that seems unethical

For more pointers read "netiquette" guides such as the one found at http://www.fau.edu:80/rinaldi/netiquette.html

---

APPLICATION: HOW TO WRITE NOT "GOOD," BUT WELL

No one writes "good" or "really good," let alone the abominable "goodly." You must aspire to write *well*, to convey your thoughts and feelings in a clear and cogent fashion. Too many students excuse their poor writing by arguing that they are "just engineers," but writing follows rules, or grammar. Writing requires creativity and structure. Writing has form and flow. Writing demands concept and precision. Writing employs books and computers. I say, then, writing *is* engineering!

Foremost in writing is *communication*. Clear expression is crucial—anyone who muddles a concept will not be understood by others. Lately, however, e-mail has come to dominate written communication,

and sloppiness pervades the medium. Don't fall prey to it: consider some of these tips for proper e-mail communication:

- *Subjects*: The subject line of an e-mail should refer to the message's general content. And keep perspective! Consider the subject line "READ IMMEDIATELY" for a message saying, "hey mike you here about what happened to sam and the photocopier?" These subject lines and messages do not inform; they just annoy. What else is wrong with that message? Also, when replying, consider whether the subject is still appropriate.

- *Salutation*: "Yo dude" or "Hey babe" or "hi boss-person!" are certainly cozy and perhaps even appropriate in certain circumstances. However, first try correctly identifying your addressee.
- *Spelling*: Consider the choice—and know the difference—between homonyms such as *affect/effect, hear/here, it's/its, than/then*, and *you're/your*. Also, many e-mail programs have built-in spell checkers. Occasionally, try using one. Did you catch the *"here/hear"* error in Mike's message under the Subjects bullet?
- *Grammar*: *i am fed up with people who simply cannot bother to punctuate capitalize insert articles and define sentences inside email like this sample see what i mean its really really annoying*
- *Everything*: *thiss sentense have manny mis-spelled word and missteaks If your writign like this than its you job too proofred you're work.* I have received too many homework solutions and e-mail messages with writing of this sort! How many mistakes can you count?

Proofreading your own work is tough, but the effort pays off. Consider investing some time and energy in developing better written communication skills. Communication is essential for *all* professions.

PRACTICE!

3. E-mail a friend. Say hello.
4. E-mail two people the same message, using `mailx person1 person2`.
5. You can e-mail a text file with the command line `mailx username < file`. Try e-mailing your `info.txt` file to yourself.
6. Read the `test2` message. Save the message into a file called `test2.txt`.

4.5 GLOBAL COMMUNICATION

Sharing TCP/IP protocols with the Internet has enhanced Unix's utility in local and global communication, enabling Unix to provide efficient programs for e-mail, file transfer, chatting, and browsing the World Wide Web. Most computers, in fact, share common protocols for transmitting, receiving, and translating information. Note that many protocols and programs have identical names. Some common protocols are introduced in this section.

4.5.1 Remote Login

The Internet provides means to access to your account from remote locations. Command lines such as `rlogin username@hostname` and `telnet hostname` allow users to remotely login from a computer outside of your usual LAN, provided the computer and your system are connected to a common WAN. Note that you must have local and remote accounts to log in. Try `telnet hostname` to access another system in your network:

STEP 31: CONNECTING TO REMOTE SYSTEM

```
dis% telnet free.buffalo.edu
```
Connect to a remote host. Do you know another system you might have access to?
```
Trying 999.999.9.999...
Connected to free.buffalo.edu.
Escape character is '^]'.
```
`telnet` reports the remote systems's IP address. You have successfully connected. In case of emergency, leave the system with ^].

```
UNIX(r) System V Release 4.0 (free.buffalo.edu)          Greetings!

login: dis                        A login prompt appears from the remote host.
Password:                                          Enter your password.

dis%                                       You can work on your remote system.
```

Logging out disconnects **telnet.**

When entering **telnet** with no hostname, you are prompted with telnet>. Then, to access a remote system, enter **open hostname**. If you make a mistake, enter **close hostname,** and try again. When done, enter **quit.** Obtain help on **telnet** by typing **?** at the prompt.

4.5.2 File Transfer

Use file transfer protocol (FTP) to transfer files across accounts and networks. The command **ftp hostname** accesses a remote site. If you have an account on such a remote site, enter your username and password. Typically, non-restricted sites permit login with the username anonymous:

STEP 32: OBTAINING FILES FROM A REMOTE HOST

```
dis% ftp explorer.arc.nasa.gov                    Access a NASA FTP server.

Connected to explorer.arc.nasa.gov              You have accessed the site.
                                             Usually, a longer message is sent.

Name (explorer.arc.nasa.gov:dis):anonymous       Log in "anonymously."
                                        Such FTP servers are called "anonymous."

331 Guest login ok, send ident as password.       NASA let you in.

Password:                Don't worry—just type your username@hostname as a password.

230 Guest login ok, access restrictions apply.

ftp> cd pub/         Usually you go to the "public" directory first. cd means "change directory."

ftp> ls              FTP employs many standard Unix commands. Isn't it great you're learning Unix?

ftp> cd space/GIFS/  Look inside a directory of pictures. GIF = Graphical Interchange Format.

ftp> ls              You will see a variety of image files. Look for files with ".gif" extensions.

ftp> binary          Change the transfer format to binary: Non-ASCII files could become gar-
                                    bled, though sometimes you can skip this step.

200 Type set to I                              FTP reports binary mode is on.

ftp> get shuttle1.gif          Transfer a picture of the Space Shuttle to your account.

Transfer information is now reported.

ftp> bye                                            Exit the FTP server.

221 Goodbye.                                    FTP is a very polite protocol.

dis%                                         You're back to your Unix prompt.
```

You can also access FTP by entering the command with no arguments. At the `ftp>` prompt, enter **open** and **close** as you did with **telnet**. To place a file into the account that you accessed, use **put** **filename**. To learn more, enter **help** at the **ftp** prompt for a list of other commands available, and refer to Appendix E for some Web sites that list FTP sites.

PRACTICE!

7. Access the NASA FTP site again. Download another picture.

8. Obtain the `pe-eit-exam` FAQ (frequently asked questions) file from the directory `/pub/usenet-by-group/news.answers/engineering` at `rtfm.mit.edu`.

4.5.3 USENET

USENET collects discussion groups that apply the network news transport protocol (NNTP). Currently, there are thousands of different groups, with one or more focusing on almost every imaginable topic. Unix programs like **trn**, which allow you to access USENET, are relatively easy to learn and apply. Many mail programs such as **pine** incorporate news readers as well. Consult your site for programs and newsgroup availability.

4.5.4 The World Wide Web

The **World Wide Web** is a grand agglomeration of electronic information accessible over the Internet and features text, graphics, and often, interactive capability. Accessing

Figure 4.6.   Web Browser

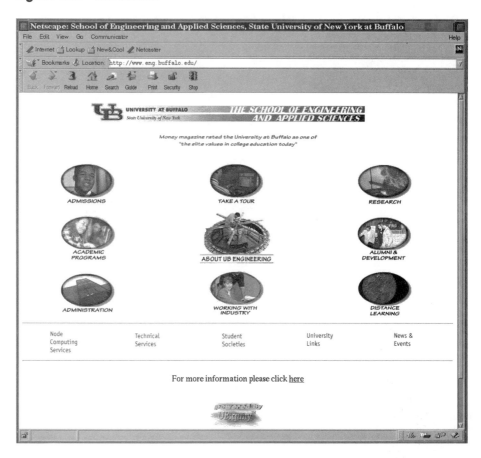

and viewing documents here is frequently referred to as "browsing the Web," as shown in Figure 4.6. Although text-based Web programs such as **lynx** strip out graphics and leave just text, most people prefer the full multimedia effect afforded by browsers such as Netscape Navigator.

Find information on the Web with a ***uniform resource locator*** (***URL***), which take the form **http://IP_Address**. The URL http://www.yrbook.com, for instance, accesses an interesting commercial site that hosts a variety of music, entertainment, and advertising (remember the domains?).

In general, URLs contain a *transfer method and location*. Consider http://www.yrbook.com. The first portion, http, indicates the method, hypertext transfer protocol (HTTP), while the rest of the URL, www.yrbook.com, corresponds to its location. URLs come in other forms, and you can specify other transfer methods as well: URLs such as **ftp://IP_Address** or **telnet://IP_Address** are acceptable, given proper IP addresses.

PRACTICE!

9. Use a Web browser to load the site http://www.asce.org/. What site have you found?

10. Use a Web browser to locate the FTP site **rtfm.mit.edu**. Download the file about-faqs. (Hint: Search /pub/usenet-by-group/news.answers.)

11. Is "www.aaes.org" in form of a URL? Does your browser still accept this as a location?

4.6 APPLICATION: COMMUNICATING WITH COWORKERS

In this section, you will use e-mail to communicate with coworkers.

4.6.1 Problem
Your project manager, Stuart, wants an update on the current version of your work.

4.6.2 Background
In Chapter 3, you developed a prototype of the hello.C program in ASCII text. The e-mail program **mailx** permits you to mail messages and files.

4.6.3 Methodology
Use the **mailx** command **~v** to edit your update. After all, you do not want something inappropriate to slip in and go to your boss! You can also use **mailx** to send your hello.C file by e-mail.

4.6.4 Solution
First, e-mail your boss. Assume that Stuart's e-mail address is "boss." Be courteous!

STEP 33: SEND A PROGRESS REPORT		
dis% **mailx boss**		*E-mail your boss. Use his e-mail address.*
Subject: **progress report**		*You are updating Stuart on your progress.*
~c dis		*Send a carbon copy of the message to yourself.*
~v		*Type ~v. Next, press **Return**. You are now in **vi**, or visual editor, mode.*
To: boss		*Some systems will let you now change message-address information.*

```
Subject: progress report                You do not need to change these settings.

Stuart,                                  Write your message.
   Work  is  progressing  well  on  hello.C.  I  had  some  minor
   bugs to contend with, but work is proceeding according to
   the schedule and within the allotted budget. I am sending
   the current program in the next message. In fact, I think
   this is some of my finest work. Can I have a raise?
   Thank you,
   Dave
:wq                           Assuming that you are in vi, "save your message and exit vi." You can enter
                                         more commands, keep typing, or send the e-mail with ^D.

^D

EOT                                             Your message has been transmitted.

dis%                                                The Unix prompt reappears.
```

Now, send him a copy of your `hello.C` program using the following Unix command line:

STEP 34: EDIT AN E-MAIL MESSAGE BEFORE SENDING

```
dis% mailx boss < hello.C         Mail a copy of the file, hello.C, to your boss.
                                  (The redirection operator, <, is discussed in Chapter 7.)

dis% mailx                                           Check your mail.

mailx version 5.0 [date] Type ? for help      mailx reports version and date.

"/var/mail/dis": 2 messages 2 unread              mailx shows your system
                                                mail directory and message counts.

>N 1 david i schwartz Fri Oct 26 9:16 27/804 progress report

 N 2 stuart t boss     Fri Oct 26 9:18 4/145 good work; no

q                                                  Enter q to quit.
```

Do not count on your boss saving your file or giving you a raise quite yet. In the next chapter, you will create directories to store backups of your work.

SUMMARY

This chapter introduced a variety of methods for using Unix in both local and global communication. Many utilities for local communication help you keep informed and stay in contact with others in your computer network. Unix and the Internet share methods of information transfer called protocols. Common protocols include e-mail, remote access, file transfer, newsgroups, and Web browsing. Uniform resource locators (URLs) for Web browsing consist of a method by which to access information and the location of where to obtain it.

KEY TERMS

domain	IP address	Internet
e-mail	local-area networks (LAN)	uniform resource locator (URL)
e-mail address	protocol	wide area network (WAN)
header	transmission control protocols/	world wide web (WWW)
hostname	Internet protocols (TCP/IP)	

Problems

1. What is the hostname for your computer system?

2. What is your full e-mail address?

3. What are two ways to find out information about yourself on your account? Hint: Use **finger** and **who** with options.

4. How many users on your system have the first name Chester?

5. What other e-mail programs are available on your system?

6. E-mail yourself and your instructor a message about your educational goals.

7. How do you find a full list of tilde escape commands from within **mailx**?

8. How would you e-mail a file using **mailx** with a line that starts with a tilde (~)? Hint: See Question 7.

9. Sometimes e-mail you send "bounces" back to you—that is, you receive notification that your message could not be delivered. Discuss some reasons why e-mail might bounce.

10. Locate a Usenet program and subscribe to an engineering-oriented newsgroup. Name at least five other engineering-oriented groups.

11. Post a message in a newsgroup. Save that message after it has been successfully posted. Print it out.

12. What is a "FAQ," according to the FAQ about FAQs? Refer to `about-faqs` from practice Problem 8.

13. Use your Web browser to locate the Unix FAQ FTP site. Download all FAQ files contained therein.

14. Project 1: Find the main URLs of the World Wide Web home pages of the following engineering organizations:

    American Institute of Aeronautics and Astronautics

    American Institute of Chemical Engineers

    The American Society of Civil Engineers

    The American Society of Mechanical Engineers

    The American Society for Engineering Education

    The Institute of Electrical and Electronics Engineers

    The Institute of Industrial Engineers

    Draft a one-paragraph, double-spaced essay about the nature of each society. Use a text editor to type your report.

15. Project 2: What other engineering organizations can you find on the Web? Draft a one- to two-paragraph, double-spaced essay about the nature of each society. Use a text editor to type your report. Hint: Find the American Association of Engineering Societies (AAES) Web site. Also, visit http://arioch.gsfc.nasa.gov/wwwvl/engineering.html.

5

Directories

5.1 DIRECTORIES

Whereas files store your "stuff," **directories** store your files. Look at Figure 5.1: Think of paper files stored inside folders or filing-cabinet drawers. Now, consider computer files as that paper, and directories as the folders and cabinet drawers. Directories can thus assist organizing a morass of files.

5.1.1 Directory Tree

Picture for a moment a tree, with its main trunk and large branches splitting off into smaller branches and twigs. Eventually, the extremities terminate with leaves. As illustrated in Figure 1.4, a **directory tree**, an organized hierarchy of files and directories, is similar. With the **root** directory (see next paragraph) forming the trunk, directories act as a tree's branches. Each time a directory is placed into another directory, the tree splits outward and downward. Think of the related files grouped together inside directories as the tree leaves.

Figure 5.2 shows a portion of a directory tree. The uppermost, or "top," directory (the trunk) in Unix is called *root* and is represented by the forward slash (/). The root directory contains *everything* on your system. Files, such as info.txt, and empty directories form the "leaves" that terminate the branches.

5.1.2 Directory Names

Directory names resemble filenames with one exception. You may use a forward slash (/) to distinguish directory names. Just append a slash at the end to indicate that the directory contains other directories. Try vocalizing directories with the slash as "the directory called *directory* contains . . . " For

OBJECTIVES

After reading this chapter, you should be able to:

- Construct a directory tree to organize your Unix account
- Illustrate principles of Unix file management
- Distinguish between relative and absolute pathnames
- Practice navigating a directory tree

Figure 5.1. Filing-Cabinet and Folder Analogies for Computer Files and Directories

instance, translate /home/chz/ as "the directory home contains the directory chz." Of course, chz/ may contain other files and directories. Beware, though, that Unix programs and references often do not bother with the "final" slash when specifying a directory. The slash is merely a convenience. For instance, /home/ and /home represent equivalent directory names.

5.1.3 Pathname

Pathnames indicate the locations of every item in the directory tree. Pathnames are composed of sequences of directories that terminate with a file or directory name: pathnames provide paths to particular data. For instance, in Figure 5.2, the path to info.txt from dis/ is dis/info.txt. Starting from root (/), the pathname is /home/dis/info.txt. Vocalize this pathname as "root contains the directory home which contains the directory dis which contains the file info.txt."

5.1.4 Parent-Child Relationship

A directory containing files or other directories is called a **parent**, while a file or directory contained inside another directory is called a **child**. The child of one directory, of course, may be a parent as well. This parent directory might yield, in turn, its own file and directory children. Hence, staying with Figure 5.2, dis/ is the child of the parent home/. The directory home/, in turn, is the child of root. Because the tree terminates with root, root is the **ancestor**, the parent of all other parents.

Figure 5.2. Example Directory Tree

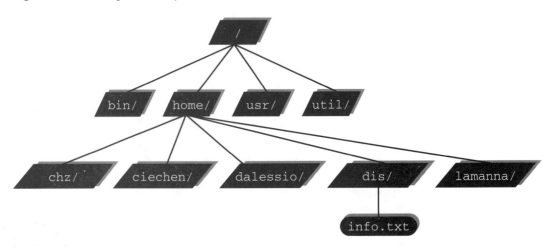

5.1.5 Absolute Pathnames

What is the "path" to my office? My "current working residence" is Buffalo, New York. More specifically, I live in the city of Buffalo located in the state of New York located in the United States of America. Expanding even further, the United States is located in North America located in the Northern Hemisphere located on the planet Earth. Indeed, someone looking for my office has quite a path to follow.

The root directory is like planet Earth, the highest level from which to specify directions.[1] An ***absolute pathname*** incorporates the complete trail to follow to a directory or file, starting from root and ending with the item of interest. In Figure 5.2, then, the file `info.txt` has the absolute pathname `/home/dis/info.txt`.

5.1.6 Relative Pathnames

Anyone who lives *inside* Buffalo does not need directions *to* Buffalo. Residents would only require directions *relative* to Buffalo. On Unix, complete directions in the form of absolute pathnames are typically unnecessary, so using shorter ***relative pathnames*** save time. A relative pathname starts at a particular directory, usually the directory from which you working, rather that at root.

For instance, imagine you are standing inside Figure 5.2's directory `home/` and viewing the contents: you would see directories `chz/`, `ciechen/`, `dalessio/`, `dis/`, and `lamanna/`. From this perspective, these directories have relative pathnames of `chz/`, `ciechen/`, and so on. Likewise, the relative pathname of `info.txt` within `home/` is simply `dis/info.txt`.

PRACTICE!

> **1.** What is the absolute pathname of `info.txt` as shown in Figure 5.2?
> **2.** What is the absolute pathname of the directory `chz/`?
> **3.** What is the relative pathname of `info.txt` if you are *inside* `dis/`?

5.2 HOME DIRECTORY

In Chapter 3, you stored files in your Unix account, or HOME. Recall that each account contains the system memory allotted to each user. When you log in, Unix places you inside your HOME directory, which is your own space that is labeled with your unique username. Most Unix systems place users' HOME directories inside a `/home/` directory, as shown in Figure 5.3. My account, `dis/`, is stored inside the directory `/home/`. Thus, my HOME has the absolute pathname `/home/dis/`.

Never confuse HOME with `home/`! Your shell sets the default value HOME, which tells Unix where your account resides. `/home/`, on the other hand, contains all other HOMEs. Recognizing that these names can be confusing, some systems store user accounts in directories with entirely different names. Where does your HOME reside? Try the **echo** command from Chapter 2:

STEP 35: DETERMINE THE ABSOLUTE PATHNAME OF HOME

```
dis% echo $HOME          Show the system-defined variable for your HOME directory.

/home/dis                Dave's account has this absolute pathname. What does your output say? Many
                         Unix commands will not display a terminal slash (/).
```

---

[1] How would you classify the Internet according to this analogy?

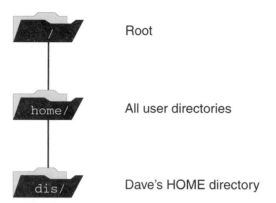

Root

All user directories

Dave's HOME directory

Figure 5.3. Example Directory Tree for Dave's Account

PRACTICE!

4. Complete the following statement;
   My **HOME** directory has the absolute pathname _____

5. Describe the parent/child relationship of your **HOME** directory with respect to your system's root.

5.3 DIRECTORY NAVIGATION

How do you access any particular directory? In this section, commands for accessing and changing directories are demonstrated.

Figure 5.4. Computers are supposed to usher in an age of the paperless office. Imagine a work environment free of memos and filing cabinets. Courtesy of Michael Lamanna.

Figure 5.5. A paperless office. Courtesy of Michael Lamanna.

5.3.1 Current Working Directory

Suppose that someone asked how to find your residence. Wouldn't you first ask from which direction he or she was coming? Knowing the person's present location helps determine directions to another location. Dealing with a directory tree is no different. The working directory—the present location—must first be known. Sometimes the working directory is called the ***current working directory*** (***CWD***).

Basically, the CWD is the absolute pathname to your current directory. Determine your current working directory with the *print working directory* command, **pwd**:

STEP 36: DETERMINE THE WORKING DIRECTORY

```
dis% pwd                          What is the absolute pathname to your working directory?

/home/dis    Current working directory is HOME. pwd does not display a terminal slash (/) on dis.
```

Try vocalizing **pwd** as "path to working directory" to remember the command.

5.3.2 Listing Directory Contents

What does HOME contain? In Chapter 3, you used the command **ls** to list the contents of HOME. You can also specify a pathname as **ls *pathname***, where ***pathname*** is either relative or absolute. If you enter no pathname, Unix assumes you mean your CWD.

STEP 37:
LIST THE
CONTENTS OF
THE WORKING
DIRECTORY
(RELATIVE
PATHNAME)

```
dis% pwd                                                    Check  CWD.

/home/dis                          Still in HOME. (Don't forget to use your own HOME.)

dis% ls                                          ls shows the contents of the CWD.

info.txt                   You should have even more files. This is just an example listing.
```

You need info.txt *for later examples. If you did not create an* info.txt *in Chapter 3, please do so now!*

Later chapters illustrate modifying **ls**'s behavior with options.

Now, try using an absolute pathname to obtain the same listing:

STEP 38:
LIST THE
CONTENTS OF
THE WORKING
DIRECTORY
(ABSOLUTE
PATHNAME)

```
dis% ls /home/dis/          FInd the contents of HOME. (Be sure to use your own path here!)

info.txt           Because the CWD is HOME, entering ls and ls /home/dis/ yield the same output.
```

Note the slash (/) following the username in this example. As previously discussed, a terminal slash is not necessary, so you could have specified **/home/username** in this example. Terminating the pathname with a slash (/) is encouraged by convention.

5.3.3 Changing Directories

Why memorize the entire tree when you can change directories with **cd**? The command **cd**, when followed by a directory name, will take you to that directory. Express the directory as a relative or absolute pathname, depending on your CWD. **cd** changes the CWD to the directory to which you are moving.

cd helps navigate through the directory tree. Try changing your CWD to the parent of your working directory:

STEP 39:
CHANGE TO
PARENT
DIRECTORY OF
HOME
(ABSOLUTE
PATHNAME)

```
dis% cd /home/                              Change to the parent directory of HOME.

dis% pwd                          Use pwd to make sure that you are indeed one level higher.

/home            Yes, the working directory is now /home/, the parent of your account directory.
```

The double-dot (..) short-cut moves your CWD up one directory in the hierarchy when specified inside a pathname:

STEP 40: **CHANGE TO** **PARENT** **DIRECTORY** **(RELATIVE** **PATHNAME)**	`dis% cd /home/dis/` *Return to HOME.* `dis% cd ..` *Change the CWD to the parent directory. Type a space after* `cd`*, but* *not between the two dots.* `dis% pwd` *Where are you?* `/home` *You are inside the parent of HOME. You moved up one directory-level.*

Moving down the tree involves a similar use of pathnames. Starting from the CWD /home, go back to your HOME directory:

STEP 41:
CHANGING TO
CHILD
DIRECTORY
(RELATIVE
PATHNAME)
	`dis% ls` *List the contents of the working directory* `/home/`*.*
	
	`bstein   chattin  ciechen  dalessio  edemaitr  lamanna  somlo`
	`camama   chz      crs      dis       jchottin  meryan   thill`
	
	Sample listing of directories inside `/home/`*. These are, of course, other users' HOME directories.*
	
	`dis% cd dis/` *Change the CWD to your HOME. Use a relative path.*
	
	`dis% pwd` *Make sure you went HOME.*
	
	`/home/dis` *Yes, the working directory is indeed HOME.*

PRACTICE!

> **6.** What is the absolute pathname of the parent directory of HOME?
>
> **7.** What is the relative pathname of the parent directory of HOME?

5.3.4 Change to Working Directory

A single dot (`.`) represents your CWD. Rarely will you specify the dot except as a place holder, but just in case, try this:

STEP 42: **CHANGE TO** **WORKING** **DIRECTORY ".".**	`dis% cd .` *Type only a single dot before pressing* **Return***.* `dis% pwd` *Where did you go?* `/home/dis` *Nowhere! You stayed exactly where you started.*

For Korn Shell users, **cd -** (that's a hyphen, or dash) will change to the previous working directory, regardless of the current working directory.

5.3.5 Changing to HOME Directories

In the above examples, Unix treats HOME directories just like any other directories. If you ever leave your HOME, remembering a few key commands will help you navigate back. Most often, just enter **cd** with no pathname. Unix will then automatically change the CWD to HOME:

STEP 43:
CHANGE
DIRECTORY TO
HOME

```
dis% cd
```
Change to your HOME with this Unix shortcut.

```
dis% pwd
```
Where are you?

```
/home/dis
```
You are inside HOME.

Another method of returning to HOME involves substituting a tilde (**~**) for **/home/username/.** Thus, to change to HOME, you would enter **cd ~/** (entering **cd ~** is acceptable as well). In this example, "**~/**" represents "**/home/dis/,**" my HOME directory.

STEP 44:
CHANGE
DIRECTORY TO
HOME WITH ~/

```
dis% cd ~/
```
Go to HOME. The tilde (~) represents your HOME pathname.

```
dis% pwd
```
Where are you?

```
/home/dis
```
You are inside HOME.

Why bother with the tilde when **cd** suffices? As discussed in later chapters, copying and moving files and directories requires pathnames. Since your work resides inside HOME, the **~** provides a useful shortcut. Bourne shell users cannot substitute the tilde for HOME. If your system rejects **~**, use the full pathname instead, or try **$HOME** as in **cd $HOME**.

Moreover, you can enter *another* user's HOME directory with **cd ~username**, where no slash is written between **~** and **username**. The pathname **~username** provides a shortcut for "the HOME directory of **username**." Thus, specifying **cd ~chattin**, for example, tells Unix to change your current working directory to /home/chattin/. Try changing your CWD to a friend's directory:

STEP 45:
CHANGE
DIRECTORY TO
ANOTHER
USER'S HOME
WITH
~username

```
dis% cd ~friend
```
Pick a friend's username to enter following ~. (This command assumes that you have access permission.)

```
dis% pwd
```
If Unix doesn't report "access denied," check your new CWD.

```
/home/friend
```
You are inside a friend's HOME directory.

Often, Unix denies access to others' HOME directories in order to protect privacy. Changing such file permissions is discussed in Chapter 8.

PRACTICE!

8. What is the meaning of the command line **cd ~**?
9. What is the meaning of the command line **cd ~/**?
10. What is the meaning of the command line **cd ~dis**?
11. What is the meaning of the command line **cd ~/dis/**? (Hint: Trick question!)

5.4 SUBDIRECTORIES

Eventually, you will gather homework, projects, mail, personal files, and perhaps even more in your HOME directory, and it could become quite cluttered. Creating ***subdirectories*** inside your account will help organize these files. Subdirectories are just child directories of parent directories or, in other words, directories inside other directories. This section introduces methods for creating directories and subdirectories inside your account.

5.4.1 Directory Naming Conventions

As previously discussed, directory naming follows the same convention as file naming, only with the one major exception: you can append a slash (/) to the end of a directory name. Name wisely: after two years of naming my directories and files A, B, C, and so on, I had to delete the entire lot out of utter confusion. Also, try to capitalize the first letter in directory names because alphabetized listing in Unix shows uppercase letters first. However, directory names do not require uppercase letters. Remember, Unix is case sensitive! The directory names BLAH/ and blah/ are *not* identical.

5.4.2 Creating Subdirectories

Now, armed with naming conventions, you can start organizing your HOME with subdirectories. Think of HOME as the filing cabinet as discussed earlier: subdirectories resemble the drawers; subdirectories within subdirectories resemble file folders. The command for making directories, **mkdir**, uses the syntax **mkdir pathname**. Because you will typically have permission to change only your personal account, work more efficiently by using **mkdir** with relative pathnames instead of absolute pathnames. For the present, organize your account with directories as shown in Figure 5.6. (Replacing, of course, the absolute path /home/dis/ with your own HOME's pathname.)

Figure 5.6.   Proposed Directory Tree for Your Account

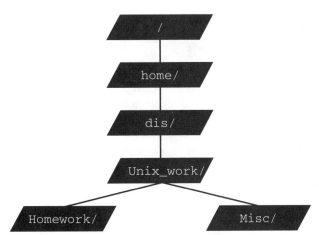

First, make a directory inside HOME called `Unix_work/`:

**STEP 46:
CREATE A
SUBDIRECTORY
WITHIN HOME**

```
dis% cd
```
First, make sure that you are in HOME.

```
dis% mkdir Unix_work/
```
Create a subdirectory called `Unix_work/`. Entering
`mkdir Unix_work` without the slash (/) produces the same results.

```
dis% ls
```
List the contents of the CWD. Did `mkdir` work?

```
Unix_work    info.txt
```
You might see more stuff listed—just focus on just these two for now.
Unix will not display a terminal slash (/) unless specifically requested
as shown in the next chapter.

Recall that entering a terminal slash is encouraged but not required. `Unix_work/` has the absolute pathname `/home/username/Unix_work/`. (Don't forget to substitute your own username!)

As indicated by Figure 5.6, you can make subdirectories within other subdirectories. For instance, your `Unix_work/` directory (a subdirectory of your HOME directory) might contain separate directories for Unix practice, homework, projects, and other things. For now, you will add two subdirectories inside `Unix_work/`: `Homework/`, to store homework solutions, and `Misc/` for other Unix work.

You can create these directories using either relative or absolute pathnames. The usual procedure involves first changing your CWD to a parent directory, then, adding new subdirectories. Building a directory tree compares to adding more drawers to your file cabinet. You label each directory, or drawer, according to the particular contents organized within that directory.

Try creating a subdirectory inside your `Unix_work/` directory:

**STEP 47:
CREATE
SUBDIRECTORY
WITHIN
ANOTHER
SUBDIRECTORY**

```
dis% cd Unix_work/
```
Go inside the `Unix_work/` directory.

```
dis% pwd
```
Check the CWD.

```
/home/dis/Unix_work
```
You are indeed inside your `Unix_work/` directory.

```
dis% mkdir Homework/
```
Create a subdirectory within `Unix_work/` called `Homework/`.

```
dis% ls
```
Ensure the directory, `Homework/`, was created.

```
Homework
```
Here is the new subdirectory. Everything is OK.

Keep track of error messages! When specifying pathnames, you should ensure that the directories you indicate actually exist. Non-existant directories will generate error messages. Use `ls` to list contents of directories and **cd** to change your CWD—and do not forget that you can view a directory's contents from just about anywhere, as long as you use a proper pathname to that directory. In fact, you could have created your directory `Homework/` from any CWD by using the absolute pathname **~/Homework**.

PRACTICE!

Create your `~/Unix_work/Misc/` subdirectory in this practice session. Refer to Figure 5.4:

12. Change your working directory to HOME.

13. List your directory contents. Did you create the `Unix_work/` directory? If not, do so now.
14. Practice changing your working directory to `Unix_work/` and back to HOME again.
15. Create another subdirectory called `Misc/` inside `Unix_work/`.
16. Did you create `~/Unix_work/Misc/`? Check by changing your working directory.
17. Change your working directory back to HOME. List the contents of your `Unix_work/` directory.

5.4.3 Removing Directories

Suppose that you created a directory called `Test/` inside `Unix_work/`, but you decide that you won't need `Test/`. Use **rmdir *pathname*** to delete *empty* directories, or directories that contain no files or subdirectories (even empty ones). Try creating and then removing an empty subdirectory:

STEP 48: REMOVING EMPTY SUB-DIRECTORIES

dis% **mkdir ~/Unix_work/Test/**	*Create a new subdirectory,* Test/, *inside* Unix_work/.
dis% **ls ~/Unix_work/**	*List the contents of* Unix_work/.
Homework Misc Test	*These are the contents of* ~/Unix_work/.
dis% **rmdir ~/Unix_work/Test/**	*Remove the subdirectory* ~/Unix_work/Test/.
dis% **ls ~/Unix_work/**	*List the contents of* Unix_work/.
Homework Misc	Test/ *no longer appears. It was deleted!*

As long as a directory has any contents at all, **rmdir** will not delete the directory. Deleting *files* is reviewed in the next chapter. Also, note that you cannot be *within* a directory that you are attempting to delete (you cannot delete your CWD).

PRACTICE!

18. Create a subdirectory called `Test2/` inside `~/Unix_work/`.
19. Change your working directory to the new subdirectory `Test2/`.
20. Try using relative pathnames to delete `Test2/`.

5.5 APPLICATION: USING SUBDIRECTORIES TO ORGANIZE FILES

In this section, you will create directories in which to store your programs.

5.5.1 Problem

Assume you spent many hours developing your `hello.C` program shown in Chapter 3. Though your company, D.I.S., Inc., treats its employees well, your client, who pays for those many hours, might not be as forgiving if you lose your work.

5.5.2 Background

Without subdirectories to organize your work, your computer account can become quite messy. Each project should have its own separate directory in which to save files.

5.5.3 Methodology

Use **cd**, **pwd**, **mkdir**, and **ls** to create and organize subdirectories. Also, consider using GUI file-management programs such as **filemgr**. (See Appendix B for more information.)

5.5.4 Solution

Create subdirectories with **mkdir**. Be sure to constantly check your directory path to ensure that your directories have proper locations:

STEP 49: CREATE SUB-DIRECTORIES TO ORGANIZE PROJECTS

`dis% cd`	*Start from CWD, your HOME.*
`dis% ls`	*List your files.*
`Unix_work   hello.C`	*This is a sample listing. You should see more files.*
`dis% mkdir PROJECTS/`	*Create a directory for programming projects.*
`dis% mkdir PROJECTS/Hello/`	*Create a subdirectory called* `Hello/`, *inside the directory* `PROJECTS/`.
`dis% mkdir PROJECTS/Backups/`	*Create a subdirectory called* `Backups/`.
`dis% cd PROJECTS/`	*Change the CWD to* `PROJECTS/`.
`dis% pwd`	*Check the CWD.*
`/home/dis/PROJECTS`	*You are inside* `~/PROJECTS/`.
`dis% ls`	*List the contents of the CWD.*
`Backups   Hello`	*You will store your programs and results inside these subdirectories.*

In the next chapter, you will move and copy pertinent files into your new project directories.

SUMMARY

This chapter introduced the basics of directories and subdirectories. A tree structure organizes directories, subdirectories, and files with "root" on top. Unix uses relative and absolute pathnames to locate everything contained in this hierarchy. Typically, users work from HOME, their personal account directories. Knowing the current working directory helps users navigate the tree. Commands such as **ls**, **cd**, **mkdir**, and **rmdir** also help navigate directories, as well as organize work. Creating a directory tree is akin to filling a filing cabinet with drawers and files that store different contents.

KEY TERMS

absolute pathname	directory	relative pathname
ancestor	directory tree	root
child	parent	subdirectory
current working directory (CWD)	pathname	

APPLICATION: HOW TO GET THE MOST OUT OF CLASS

There is a very simple secret to performing well on homework and tests: *Go to class!*

- *Go to class*: Consider the following questions: Where will the assignment be posted? What material does the homework cover? What material will you be tested on? Now, what's the answer in each case? *Go to class*. On an assignment due date, very often a student asks, "When is the homework due?" Usually, I look at my watch and retort, "In about five minutes." *Go to class*.

- *Learn before you learn*: Part of classroom boredom arises from complete bafflement. Most of us cannot pay attention for lengthy periods of time, and when unprepared, chances for absorption are slim at best. However, skimming the textbook ahead of time helps. After all, learning is often a function of repetition. (*Go to class!*) For this text, even *attempting* commands beforehand will ease laboratory instruction.

- *Listen*: Most students prefer taking notes in class—writing *anything* seems preferable to falling asleep. There's nothing really wrong with taking notes; the problem is doing so indiscriminately. Did you know that some students, and not necessarily the naturally gifted, can pass difficult classes without ever taking a single note? Their trick is *listening*. What your professor *says*, and how he or she says it, is often the indicator of what he or she judges most important to know. Guess what usually shows up on tests?

- *Take notes*: Combine listening with note taking. Let your professor's voice guide your writing. Also, combine what your professor discusses in class with any written notes he or she might distribute.

- *Ask questions*: What portions of the text seemed most confusing during your skimming? Has the professor reached that portion of the text? If so, has the material been clarified? No? Raise your hand! You can ask an insightful question because you previously reviewed the material. But even if your question won't be insightful, or if you're not sure, ask anyway. Chances are that more than half the class is wondering the same thing.

- *Now, go to class!*

Problems

1. Is the directory name `1_2_3_4/` acceptable? Why or why not?

2. What are two names for the uppermost directory in Unix?

3. What does "current working directory" mean? How do you tell Unix to report your current working directory?

4. Assume that your current working directory is `/home/chz/Data/`. What is the absolute pathname of the parent directory?

5. Assume that your current working directory is `/home/chz/Data/`. Which directory in this path is a child of `chz/`? Specify a relative pathname.

6. What are two ways, not including absolute pathnames, of listing your current working directory?

7. Can you view the contents of a directory with **more?** Why or why not?

8. Assume that your working directory is HOME. What are three ways of listing the contents of HOME using **ls** and only one command line?

9. Assume that your working directory is root. What is your working directory if you enter the command **cd ..**?

10. What is the relative pathname of root for your system? Start from HOME.

11. What command line will change your CWD to a friend's HOME directory? Assume that your working directory is your own HOME, and that your friend has the username `rogil`. Show both absolute and relative pathname methods of changing the CWD.

12. Assume that the text file `info.txt` has the path `/home/dis/Unix_work/info.txt`. Assume also that your working directory is *your* HOME, not `dis/`. Show how to view the contents of `info.txt`, using just one command line with an absolute pathname.

13. Describe a sequence of command lines using only relative pathnames with which you could view the same `info.txt` file described in Problem 12. Hint: There are several ways to achieve the same goal. Assume `dis`'s account allows access for **cd** and **ls**.

14. C Shell and Korn Shell users only: What are four ways of returning to your HOME directory from another directory with just one command line and one use of **cd**? Hint: Think of two ways in which the tilde (~) can be used.

15. Assume that you create an empty subdirectory, `Empty/`, in HOME. First, you enter **cd ~/ Empty**, then **rmdir ./**. What happens? Why?

16. Make a subdirectory in your account called `C/`. Now make a subdirectory `B/` within `C/`. Finally, make a subdirectory `A/` inside `B/`. What is the absolute pathname of `A/`? Be sure to show the sequence of command lines you entered.

17. Delete all of the directories that you created in Problem 15. Be sure to set your current working directory to an appropriate directory. Show the sequence of command lines required for this procedure.

18. Project: Suppose that you are coordinating a project to design *widgets*. As project manager, you need to organize various tasks, including research, scheduling, analysis, and inspection. What other tasks might be associated with a large design project? Identify various categories of project work, and think of at least two other subtasks associated with each. For instance, analysis might involve choosing software, developing test cases, and determining results. Create directories and subdirectories for these tasks and subtasks. Provide thorough examples of your command line sequences, and edit your report with a text editor. Draw a directory tree that depicts your organization.

6

File Management

6.1 FILE LISTING REVISITED

Listing directory contents helps you manage your account. You can modify **ls** with many options, such as **-F** and **-a**, both of which this chapter introduces. Later chapters discuss other useful options.

6.1.1 Hidden Files

Certain files often sit unchanged for long periods. System-configuration files, for instance, are rarely edited. Thus, there is little reason to list them every time you invoke **ls**. Such files "hide" from **ls** by preceding their filenames with a dot (**.**). Typical *hidden files* such as .cshrc and .login configure account variables and assist log in procedures. To have **ls** list all files, including hidden files, use the option **-a** before the *pathname*. You would enter **ls -a *pathname***:

OBJECTIVES

After reading this chapter, you should be able to:

- Use more Unix file-management commands
- Use more-refined options for listing directory contents
- Duplicate and rename files and directories
- Apply notions of relative and absolute pathnames to reorganizing files

STEP 50:
LIST ALL FILES

```
dis% ls /home/dis/                          Use regular file-listing command.

Unix_work   info.txt                 Normally "visible" files and directories are shown.

dis% ls -a /home/dis/                  List all files inside your HOME directory.

.  ..  .cshrc  .login  Unix_work  info.txt        Hey, there are more files!
```

You might have even more files listed. Did you notice that the directories "**.**" and "**..**" also appear? Never forget that you can access working and parent directories from the current working directory.

6.1.2 File Types

Eventually, you may forget whether a name corresponds to a file or directory. In Step 50, for example, **ls** makes no distinction between Unix_work, a directory, and info.txt, a file. How can you tell the difference? Remedy this problem with the ***file type*** option, **-F**. The command line **ls -F *pathname*** will list the directory's contents along with their types:

STEP 51:
LIST TYPES

```
dis% ls -F /home/dis/              List contents with types inside your HOME directory.

Unix_work/  info.txt         Because Unix_work is a directory, the slash (/) is appended
                                                                    to the name.
```

ls -F indicates directories, such as Unix_work, by adding a slash (/) at the end of their names. Files are listed with no additional characters. When you use **-F**, you might turn up other characters, such as *, for *executables*, and @, for *links*. These and more are discussed in later chapters.

Many command options can be combined in a single line. Using both **-a** and **-F** with **ls** will list all files with their types:

STEP 52:
LIST CONTENTS WITH TYPES

```
dis% ls -a -F /home/dis/          List all files with their types inside your HOME directory.

./ ../ .cshrc .login Unix_work/ info.txt      File types are indicated for all files.
                                               You might have even more files listed.
```

The command lines **ls -aF *pathname*** and **ls -Fa *pathname*** are acceptable shortcuts. In general, command options can be reversed except in special cases, as discussed in Chapter 7.

PRACTICE!

1. Change to your HOME directory. List all files contained in **HOME**, along with their types.
2. Create a file called .delete_me inside HOME. List the contents of **HOME** such that .delete_me is shown. View the contents of .delete_me.
3. List the contents along with types in your Unix_work/Misc/ directory. (This directory is created in Chapter 5.)

Figure 6.1.   Super computers don't have to be expensive—imagine "no-cost" parallel supercomputing! Using donated, junked PCs and freely available Linux, these scientists created a powerful super computer. Courtesy of Stuart Chen.

6.2 BASIC FILE COPYING AND RENAMING

Chapter 5 discussed file management in terms of assembling a filing cabinet for your stuff. Just as with a filing cabinet, sometimes you need to reorganize your directories. The Unix *copy* and *move* commands, **cp** and **mv**, can help you do that. This section introduces copying and renaming files within the same current working directory.

6.2.1 Copying Files

Suppose that you need to add text to `info.txt`, but do not want to lose your original file. Copying the file first would create an untouched version as a ***backup***. This copy of `info.txt` would have contents identical to the original.

The Unix command for *copy* is **cp**, with the syntax **cp *source target***. Both ***source*** and ***target*** are pathnames. (So as not to complicate matters, for now, assume the CWD contains both files.) Think of ***source*** as the old (original) file and ***target*** as the desired duplicate. As the command states, Unix copies the contents of ***source*** into a newly created file, ***target***. Choose a new filename for ***target***, but make sure that the name does not repeat on already present in the CWD. Otherwise, ***target*** might overwrite the pre-existing file.

Try copying the contents of `info.txt` into a new file, `new_info.txt`, with the command **cp**:

STEP 53:
COPY A FILE

```
dis% cp info.txt new_info.txt
```

Copy your `info.txt` *file. Remember to type the underscore (_)!*

```
dis% ls
```
Unix will return the prompt if **cp** *succeeds. Now list your files—it's always good to check.*

```
info.txt  new_info.txt
```
The copy of info.txt, new.info.txt, *is listed.*

On many systems, **cp** and other similar commands prompt for "yes/no" responses before working. Such a prompt in response to a command indicates that the command has been *aliased*. Aliases customize and rename commands with various options. Many commands, like **cp** as described above, include an ***interactive option***, **-i**, to confirm or cancel instructions. In general, unless you *know* that your system provides interactive aliases, you should use **cp -i** to copy files. See Chapter 8 for more information on command aliases.

6.2.2 Renaming Files

Filenames are fleeting. What seems perfect today may become utterly useless tomorrow. In a pinch, p1 works well as a program name. But, two years in the future you will likely forget what p1 actually does! Renaming files and directories, accomplished with the **mv**, or ***move***, command helps improve organization.

mv actually works like **cp**, except that **mv** does not preserve the original file. Entering **mv *oldname newname*** instructs Unix to make a copy of ***oldname***, name the copy ***newname***, and then delete ***oldname***. If a file called ***newname*** already exists, **mv** will write over that file. Once more, using the interactive option, **-i**, will protect your files.

APPLICATION: HOW TO LEARN COMPUTER COMMANDS

Many people complain that Unix is cryptic. After all, why couldn't the listing command, **ls**, be "list" instead? Well, it could have been—but more important matters dominated when the command was born. Recall that Unix was designed when saving memory was of supreme importance. A bit and byte saved here and there made all the difference. Now, many years later, too many applications have been built around the original command suite for sweeping changes to be made. But even if destiny chose another path, you probably would get sick of typing "list" anyway.

People *do* invent easier operating systems, but few ever manage to thrive in the marketplace. Until one does, review these tricks to understand and memorize important Unix commands:

- *Translation*: Commands usually abbreviate longer names—**ls** abbreviates *list,* **mv** abbreviates *move,* **cp** abbreviates *copy,* and so forth. Always try to find such English equivalents.
- *Syntax*: Every command has *syntax,* specific structure for command input and manner of usage. You must follow the syntax to obtain the results you desire. For example, distinguish two common uses of **ls** by their syntax: entered alone, **ls** lists the contents of the current working directory, but entered as **ls *directory*,** **ls** lists the contents of ***directory***. Similarly, the command **cp** follows the syntax, **cp *source target*,** whereby **cp** duplicates the contents of ***source*** into ***target***—and the order of the pathnames cannot be reversed. Memorize syntax for commands whenever possible.

- *Vocalization*: Do you notice how I convert command syntax into sentences? Try making a sentence out of **cp** syntax. "Copy the contents of the original file, ***source***, into a new file, ***target***." Try repeating this sort of sentence for other commands until the meaning sinks in.
- *Practice*: Practice the command **cp** with actual files. Try testing the results by viewing contents of both files. (You should see no difference between either file.) Practice using your commands, by themselves and with options,

especially right after learning them. By repetition, commands will become effortless.

- *Memorization*: A full sentence improves understanding but is difficult to memorize, so try shortening your vocalizations of commands. For instance, rather than the long sentence above, say "**cp** copies one file into another." Eventually, "**cp** duplicates files" might suffice.

Practice each method of comprehension until you feel comfortable. Keep trimming down your vocal translations until the commands become second nature. If you run into problems, you can access Unix's on-line help with the command **man command** (discussed further in the next chapter). Soon you will impress your friends and family by deciphering "cryptic" Unix!

Try changing the name of new_info.txt to new_info2.txt:

STEP 54:
RENAME A FILE

```
dis% mv new_info.txt new_info2.txt          Rename new_info.txt.

dis% ls                                      List your files again.

info.txt   new_info2.txt          new_info2.txt has replaced new_info.txt.
```

In Step 54, the files involved, new_info.txt and new_info2.txt, were specified with relative pathnames. Using absolute pathnames, you could have entered the command line **mv ~/new_info.txt ~/new_info2.txt** to perform the same action.

Why the term "move"? Because **mv** changes the pathname of the file you are duplicating. The file's new pathname represents a new *location* on the directory tree! The new pathname can even reflect storage in a new directory as demonstrated later in this chapter.

PRACTICE!

4. View the contents of info.txt and new_info2.txt.
5. Are the contents of these two files the same? Why or why not?

6.2.3 Deleting Files

Frankly, all of these text files are annoying. How do you solve the problem? **Deleting** files and directories removes their contents and names from the directory tree. Rid your account of unneeded "stuff" with the **remove** command, **rm**, which uses the syntax **rm filename**. Clean your account by removing new_info2.txt:

STEP 55:
REMOVE
A FILE

```
dis% rm new_info2.txt          Remove the file new_info2.txt from your account.

dis% ls                        Did you actually get rid of new_info2.txt?

info.txt                       new_info2.txt is indeed gone.
```

Be careful! There is no "undelete" command, so once you have removed a file, the file is gone forever! For safety, use the interactive version of remove, **rm -i** (your system might even be configured or, aliased, to do this automatically). Try an interactive remove:

STEP 56:
INTERACTIVELY
REMOVE FILES

dis% **rm -i info.txt**	*Should you delete* new_info.txt *file?*
rm: remove info.txt (yes/no)? **n**	*Answer "no"! Type* **n** *and press* **Return**.
dis% **ls**	*Are all of your files still here?*
info.txt	*Yes, all of your files are still here.*

Never forget that both **cp** and **mv** can use the interactive option **-i** to prevent overwriting files. Once overwritten, the original file disappears forever!

PRACTICE!

> **6.** Do you have the files big.txt and test.txt from previous exercises? If so, delete them. If not, create them. Now, delete them. (Practice makes perfect!)
>
> **7.** Confirm that the files big.txt and test.txt are no longer in your HOME directory.

6.3 REORGANIZING FILES

Are you superstitious? An old adage states that the more critical your work, the more likely your system will crash. Thus, you should frequently save and back up your work. You can make backups with the copy command, **cp**, but all those copies will eventually clutter your account. In this section, techniques for reorganizing your files into different, clutter-free directories are shown.

6.3.1 Copying Files into Another Directory

In the previous section that discusses copying, renaming, and deleting, you did not worry about pathnames because the current working directory was HOME. Reorganizing files into subdirectories other than the CWD, however, requires you to specify pathnames. To demonstrate how to organize your account, you will reconfigure your present directory tree (Figure 6.2). Ultimately, you will produce the tree shown in Figure 6.3.

Figure 6.2. Current Directory Tree

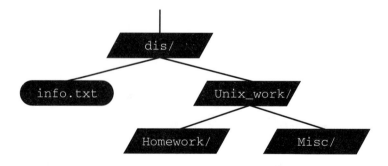

First, copy info.txt into Unix_work/Misc/. Recall the syntax, **cp *source target***, and that you can express both pathnames as either relative or absolute. Try creating a duplicate info.txt using absolute pathnames:

STEP 57:
USING
ABSOLUTE
PATHNAMES TO
COPY FILES

dis% **cp /home/dis/info.txt /home/dis/Unix_work/Misc/info.txt**

Copy info.txt *from HOME into* Unix_work/Misc/.

dis% **ls /home/dis/Unix_work/Misc/**   *List your files (using an absolute pathname).*

info.txt   *A copy of* info.txt *has been created in* ~/Unix_work/Misc/. *You could also have checked this by changing to* ~/Unix_work/Misc/ *and then typing* **ls**.

The file, info.txt, is now duplicated and stored along the new pathname, /home/ *username*/Unix_work/Misc/info.txt. The original file remains in HOME.

Do not forget that the tilde (**~**) can abreviate **$HOME**, like **/home/*username***. Entering **cp ~/info.txt ~/Unix_work/Misc/info.txt** would have also copied info.txt. In addition, if your file will retain the same name in the file's new location, repeating the name in *target* is unnecessary. Thus, in Step 57, you could have entered **cp ~/info.txt ~/Unix_work/Misc/** to copy info.txt into ~/Unix_ work/Misc/.

Now, try using relative pathnames to copy a file "upward" in the tree. Refer to Figure 6.3 to visualize the directions of your movement:

STEP 58:
USING
RELATIVE
PATHNAMES TO
COPY FILES

dis% **cd**   *Make sure that your CWD is HOME.*

dis% **cp Unix_work/Misc/info.txt info2.txt**   *Using relative pathnames.*
Copy info.txt *to* info2.txt *inside HOME.*
Because your CWD is HOME, prefixes such as ~ *and*
/home/*username* *are unnecessary.*

dis% **ls**   *List files inside the CWD, which is currently HOME.*

info.txt   info2.txt   *These files have duplicate contents.*
You chose info2.txt *so as to not overwrite* info.txt.

If you prefer absolute pathnames, **cp ~/Unix_work/Misc/info.txt ~/ info2.txt** would produce the same results. Now, your tree resembles Figure 6.3.

Figure 6.3. Target Directory Tree

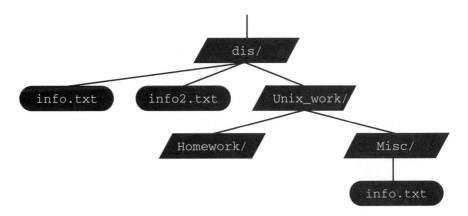

PRACTICE!

6.3.2 Moving Files into Another Directory

Now, try moving a file into another directory instead of copying the file. Do not forget that **mv** works by changing one pathname into another. As discussed previously, since a pathname reflects a directory location and name, **mv** moves files and directories. To demonstrate moving files, you will reorganize your account to look like Figure 6.4.

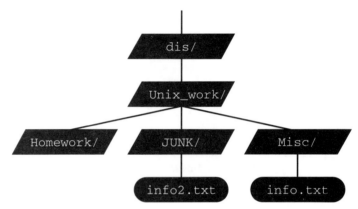

Figure 6.4. Directory Tree after Moving Files

First, make a directory for more experiments. Call it JUNK/. Recall the make-directory command line, **mkdir *pathname*:**

STEP 59: **MAKING SUB-DIRECTORIES**	dis% **cd**	*Confirm that the CWD is HOME.*
	dis% **mkdir Unix_work/JUNK/**	*Create subdirectory* JUNK/ *inside* Unix_work/.
	dis% **ls -F Unix_work/**	*List contents with types of directory* Unix_work/.
	Homework/ JUNK/ Misc/	*You have three subdirectories inside* Unix_work/.

Now, you will move `info2.txt` out of HOME and into the new JUNK/ directory. First, change your current working directory to Unix_work/. From this CWD, the relative pathname to JUNK/ is just JUNK/:

STEP 60: **MOVE FILES**	dis% **cd Unix_work/**	*Change your CWD to* Unix_work/.
	dis% **mv ~/info2.txt JUNK/**	*Move* info2.txt *out of HOME into* JUNK/. *You could also enter* **mv ../info2.txt JUNK/**.
	dis% **ls JUNK/**	*List contents of* JUNK/.
	info2.txt	*It worked!* info2.txt *was moved to this location.*

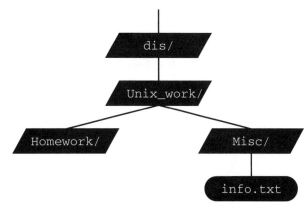

Figure 6.5. Final Organization of Directory Tree

Specifying JUNK/info2.txt as the new pathname was unnecessary, because you were not changing info2.txt's filename.

6.3.3 Cleaning House

Now, practice cleaning house by removing unnecessary files in your account, namely, JUNK/ and its contents. When finished, your new tree will look like Figure 6.5. Remember that before you can delete a directory, empty all of its contents:

STEP 61: REMOVING SUB-DIRECTORIES CONTAINING FILES

```
dis% rm ~/Unix_work/JUNK/info2.txt            Delete your info2.txt file.

dis% rmdir ~/Unix_work/JUNK/                  Delete the JUNK/ subdirectory.
```

Because the CWD is ~/Unix_work/, you could have also used relative pathnames, as in **rm JUNK/info2.txt** and **rmdir JUNK/**, to remove these items.

Removing files and directories via the two-step process in Step 61 is tedious. Chapter 8 introduces *recursive* removing, which allows you to remove entire directories along with their contents in one step. Chapter 8 also explores modifications to **cp** and **mv** as well.

PRACTICE!

11. Create a subdirectory called DELETE_ME/ inside ~/Unix_work/Misc/.

12. Change your current working directory to the new DELETE_ME/ directory.

13. Copy info.txt into ~/Unix_work/Misc/, renaming it info_copy.txt.

14. Move info_copy.txt into the new DELETE_ME/ directory. (Hint: What's the relative pathname of the CWD?)

15. Now, delete the directory DELETE_ME/.

6.4 APPLICATION: BACKING UP YOUR WORK

In this application excercise, you will back up your programs inside directories that you created using methods from this chapter.

6.4.1 Problem

You need to move your `hello.C` file into your `~/PROJECTS/Hello/` subdirectory, and create backup copies of `hello.C` as well. Then, you should remove the version from HOME to keep your account clean.

6.4.2 Background

Inevitably, at some point you will lose files, whether by accidentally deleting them or through a system crash. Once gone, Unix can not return them: most versions of Unix do not feature "undelete" commands. Although system administrators typically periodically back up system work, they cannot guarantee restoration of the most recent version. Thus, you should *always* backup your work!

6.4.3 Methodology

In general, you should use **cp** to copy files from one directory to another. If you use **mv**, be sure that the command line contains no typos, because **mv** deletes the original pathname. For **cp**, **mv**, and **rm** commands, employ the interactive option, **-i**, to prevent disastrous errors.

6.4.4 Solution

Habitually keep track of your current working directory—as long as you know your CWD, you can specify relative pathnames to save time when copying, moving, or removing:

STEP 62:
BACK UP YOUR
PROGRAMS

```
dis% cd ~/PROJECTS/                          Start from inside your PROJECTS/ subdirectory.

dis% cp -i ../hello.C Hello/            Copy your hello.C file from HOME into the
                                        Hello/ subdirectory. HOME is currently your parent directory!

dis% cp -i ../hello.C Backups/hello.C.backup       Copy your hello.C file
                                                   into the Backups/ subdirectory. Simultaneously,
                                                   rename the backup copy to hello.C.backup.

dis% more Hello/hello.C                      View the contents of the copied file.
                                             The contents of hello.C are displayed.

dis% more Backups/hello.C.backup The duplicated contents of hello.C are displayed.

dis% rm -i ~/hello.C              If your copying was successful, delete the original version.
                                  Note the -i interactive confirm option.

rm: remove ~/hello.C (yes/no)? y                           Confirm deletion.

dis% cd Backups/             Change your CWD to the Backups/ subdirectory.

dis% pwd                                                   Check your CWD.

/home/dis/PROJECTS/Backups                          OK, everything is fine.

dis% mv hello.C.backup hello.C.01          Rename the backup file with a more
                                           reasonable name. Try version numbers.

dis% cd                                                    Return to HOME.
```

In the next chapter, you will compile your `hello.C` program—and then run it!

SUMMARY

In this chapter, you practiced organizing your computer account. The basic directory commands, **cd** (change directory), **ls** (list directory contents), **mkdir** (make directory), **pwd** (print working directory), and **rmdir** (remove directory) help build and navigate directories inside Unix. The commands **cp** (copy), **mv** (move), and **rm** (remove) help organize files and directories for routine file management. The commands **cp** and **mv** have similar syntax but different function: whereas **cp** copies files, **mv** moves files. Both can rename the files on the new pathnames. For all commands, knowing absolute and relative pathnames is crucial for success.

KEY TERMS

backup	hidden file	remove
delete	interactive option	
file type	move	

Problems

1. What does the command line **ls -aF** produce? Would entering **ls -Fa** change the output?
2. What is the difference between Unix commands **cp** and **mv**?
3. Is the command line **cp test1 test1** valid for file test1? Why or why not?
4. What is the command to see the contents with types in root?
5. Create a file called ._test.txt inside your HOME directory. What command line would you enter to view the file contents of ._test.txt? How would you view all of the contents of your HOME directory?
6. Will the command lines **cp file1 file2** and **cp ./file1 ./file2** produce different results?
7. Create a text file test1.txt, and subdirectory called TEST/ inside HOME. Set your current working directory to HOME. Move test1.txt inside TEST/. Change your current working directory to TEST/. Copy test1.txt to test2.txt in HOME without changing directories.

Consider the following for Problems 8-14: Suppose that your username is edemaitr, and that all user accounts on your system are stored in /home/. You want to obtain files from your instructor, whose username is jdelmar. All of jdelmar's files are stored in the parent directory /home/jdelmar/Class/, and all files and directories are completely accessible for copying. Your system employs either a C or Korn Shell.

8. What are three different command lines that will list all the contents of /home/jdelmar/ Class/, assuming that your CWD is HOME? (Hints: One is relative, one is absolute, and another uses a tilde shortcut.)
9. How would you set the CWD to /home/jdelmar/Class/? How would you now list the contents of the CWD?
10. Working from HOME, how would you copy a file called /home/jdelmar/Class/ vortex.ps to your HOME directory using only one command line?
11. Working from the CWD /home/jdelmar/Class/, how would you use a relative pathname to copy the file vortex.ps to your HOME directory?
12. Working from CWD of ~jdelmar/Class/, how would you copy the file called /home/ jdelmar/Class/vortex.ps to your ~/Unix_work/ subdirectory?
13. What does the command line **cp ~jdelmar/Class/vortex.ps ~/** do?
14. What does the command line **cp ~jdelmar/Class/vortex.ps ~/v1.ps** do?
15. Project: Organize your account such that the pathname ~/Unix_work/Chap/A/B/C/ is viable. Store three text files called a1, b1, and c1 in subdirectory C/. Now, store three text files called a2, b2, and c2 inside ~/Unix_work/. Move a1 and a2 to A/, b1 and b2 to B/, and c1 and c2 to C/. Write a list of all your command lines.

7

Unix Tools and Utilities

7.1 UNIX TOOLS

Unix provides a rich and bountiful collection of **tools**, which are modular, relatively small, and concise programs devised for specific tasks. Unix also provides means for customizing and modifying the behavior of these programs.

The following general areas categorize Unix commands: general purpose and utility, file manipulation and file system, text processing and formatting, archiving and printing, communication and the Internet, graphics and GUIs, system administration, and programming and shell scripts. The sheer number of Unix tools can prove daunting—Unix supplies literally hundreds of commands and options from which to choose. Don't worry, though! You will most likely use only the common commands demonstrated in this text, because file management alone forms the bulk of your necessary Unix study. Occasionally, however, you *will* need obscure commands. Knowing where and how to find them are important skills introduced in this chapter.

7.2 SHELLS

Shells were introduced in Chapter 1. Of all Unix programs, the shell is the most important. Your shell activates each time you log on, and is constantly present, interpreting Unix commands.

7.2.1 Shell Functions

A Unix shell has many responsibilities:

- Prompting for command-line input: Shells help you communicate with Unix. The shell awaits input with a prompt.

OBJECTIVES

After reading this chapter, you should be able to:

- Illustrate the categories of Unix programs
- Explore uses for a very important utility, the Unix shell
- Illustrate how shells interpret and process command lines
- Understand general command-line syntax
- Find on-line help
- Understand multitasking and process management

- Interpreting your commands: Shells analyze and validate your command usage and syntax, as well as interpret any customizing and shortcuts. Shells keep track of where your "**.**" and "**..**" reside when your current working directory changes.

- Redirecting Input/Output: Shells must interpret commands to determine which devices and files should accept input and produce output. As discussed in Section 7.3, sometimes entire files act as input and output for commands.

Other duties of the shell include connecting tools together in command lines and warning you about improper command lines. Always pay attention to these warnings! Shells also allow you to develop shell scripts, customized Unix tools created with shell programming languages. View configuration files such as `.cshrc`, `.login`, and `.kshrc` for example shell scripts.

7.2.2 Shell Types

The System V Release 4 version of Unix (SVR4) provides three main shells: the *Bourne Shell* (**sh**), the *C Shell* (**csh**), and the *Korn Shell* (**ksh**). The C Shell, originally developed by Berkeley Software Distribution, is quite popular. The Korn Shell is a more advanced Bourne shell, the original Unix shell, and incorporates many C Shell features. Other popular shells include the Bourne Again Shell (**bash**, from GNU), the T Shell (**tcsh**, developed at Cornell University), and others that are available via the Internet. Which shell should you choose? Usually your system administrator determines a default user shell. Use the **echo $SHELL** command line from Chapter 2 to discover your shell. The commands **sh**, **csh**, **ksh**, **bash**, and **tcsh** spawn the shell programs.

7.3 COMMAND-LINE SYNTAX

Thus far, you have modified Unix commands with options like adding **-a** to **ls** to produce a directory all contents listing. Most Unix tools offer command-line options. Options add certain little twists to the command without altering its essential function. Changing input and output methods can further modify command lines. This section reviews these modifications of command behavior.

7.3.1 Modifying Command Behavior

In general, a Unix command including options has the form ***command options arguments***, as shown in Figure 7.1, in which a printer (ntx) other than the system-defined default printer is chosen to handle the file chapter7.ps. The option employed is **-d**.

Figure 7.1.   Command Syntax Example

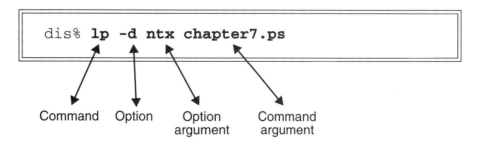

Shells separate commands, options, and arguments into separate components, parsing them according to syntactical rules. Be sure to always type a space between options, commands, and arguments! Typically, command options are indicated by their initial dashes (**-d**, **-a**, **-f**). However, some command options, such as "**n**" in **mesg n**, do not use the dash.

Sometimes options even take their own arguments. Certain **lp** options, for instance, require arguments: the option **-t** tells **lp** to print a title on banner pages of printouts and thus needs a corresponding title (**-t** *title*). Consider the command line **lp -d ntx -t DAVE chapter7.ps**. This command line prints the file, chapter7.ps on ntx with the title DAVE. Always keep options and option-arguments next to each other! For instance, entering **lp -d info.txt ntx** would cause Unix to attempt to print a file call "ntx" on printer "info.txt". (Technically, Unix does not require spaces between options and option-arguments. Now, forget I told you!)

Combine options without arguments in any order in the command line. No spaces between the options are necessary: you need only a single dash preceding them. Thus, for example, **ls -aF ~dis** or **ls -Fa ~dis** produce equivalent output because neither **-a** nor **-F** requires arguments.

PRACTICE!

1. Identify each element in the command line **ls -a /home/jchottin/**.
2. Do common shells permit more than one space between commands and arguments?
3. With **lp**, the option **-m** tells Unix to e-mail you when finished printing. This option takes no arguments. Is the command line **lp -md** *printer file* acceptable?

7.3.2 Redirecting Input/Output

Unix commands can accept and produce a variety of ***Input*** and ***Output***, or ***I/O***, as shown in Figure 7.2. The shell controls ***standard I/O***, or how input and output are transferred in response to commands. But, not all input arrives from keyboard commands, and not all output appears on a monitor. Occasionally, input and output are *redirected* from or to another source. Most commonly, the keyboard provides input, and the monitor displays output.

Changing the method of I/O is called ***redirection***. The versatile *concatenation* (linking) command, **cat**, which creates, views, and appends text files, helps demonstrate principles of I/O redirection. First, use **cat** to check your info.txt file inside **~/Unix_work/Misc/**. (Create the file if you have not already done so.)

With no options, **cat** *file* will simply view *file*:

STEP 63: VIEW TEXT FILES WITH cat

dis% **cd ~/Unix_work/Misc/**	*Work inside your* Misc/ *subdirectory. (Refer to Figure 6.3.)*
dis% **cat info.txt**	*View the text file* info.txt. *Refer to previous chapters for these subdirectories and the file.*

You will see the contents of info.txt *quickly scroll by on the monitor.*

In this instance, **cat** accepted keyboard input and displayed output on the monitor.

Now, you will change, or *redirect,* **cat**'s output to another file. Unix uses the right angle bracket (>) to redirect output. Thus, the syntax **cat > ** *file* tells **cat** to send output to *file*: all output is stored inside *file* and will not appear on the monitor. Where does **cat** find input? You supply it:

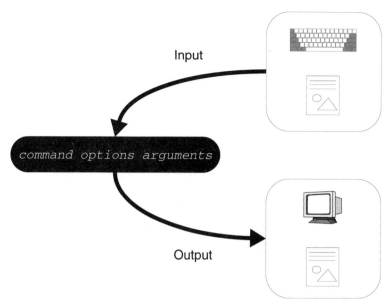

Figure 7.2. Standard Input/Output examples include methods such as keyboard entry, file input, file output, and monitor display

STEP 64:	dis% `cat > out1.txt`	*Redirect output of* **cat** *to file called* out1.txt.
REDIRECT		
OUTPUT	`Hello, I am using cat,`	*Start typing. Press* **Return** *at the line's end.*
FOR cat	`a rather interesting Unix tool.`	*Type this line. Then, press* **Return**.
	`Now, I am going to exit.`	*Type this line. Then, press* **Return**.
	`^D`	*Now, press* **^D** *to exit.*
	dis%	*Your prompt returns when Unix is finished.*

Why bother with **cat > file**? First, consider that *you* provide the input. Second, note that the output goes to a file. Guess what? You have a quick and dirty text editor!

Output redirection usually employs the syntax **command > file**, where **file** will contain the output of the preceding command line. Do not choose a filename that already exists. Shells typically warn you with error messages when attempting to over-write existing files. (For fun, look for noclobber in your system configuration files, .cshrc or .kshrc.)

Unix redirects input with the left angle bracket (<). The command line **command < file** uses entire files as input. Try redirecting input for **cat**:

STEP 65:	dis% `cat < out1.txt`	*Redirect the file* out1.txt *as input to* **cat**.
REDIRECT		
INPUT	`Hello, I am using cat,`	*You see the exact same output as if you just viewed* out1.txt.
FOR cat	`a rather interesting Unix tool.`	*So, this method is somewhat redundant.*
	`Now, I am going to press to exit.`	*Try* **cat out1.txt** *for the same results.*
	dis%	*Your prompt returns when Unix is finished.*

The command lines **cat *file*** and **cat < *file*** differ very little. A more common use of input redirection, mailing entire files, employs the left angle bracket (<). To mail ***file*** to ***username***, enter **mailx *username* < *file***.

Remembering the difference between **<** and **>** is difficult. To help, think of the redirection operators **<** and **>** as arrows "shooting" input in either direction. Thus ***command* < *file*** would "shoot" ***file*** *into* ***command***, while ***command* > *file***, would "shoot" ***file*** *out of* ***command***. (You might even pretend you could replace "<" with "←," and ">" with "→".)

You can combine both redirection methods. For example, many programs require large amounts of user entry. Storing commands and data in files improves efficiency. The syntax, ***command* < *inputfile* > *outputfile***, sends ***inputfile*** into ***command*** for processing, with the output then stored inside ***outputfile***.

Another useful related ouput redirection option is the double right angle bracket (>>). Enter ***command* >> *file*** to append redirected output of ***command*** to ***file***. Hence, **cat >> *file*** will append keyboard entry to the end of ***file***.

PRACTICE!

4. Change your current working directory to HOME. Send the CWD as redirected input to **ls**. Compare using **ls** with and without input redirection.

5. Output a listing of ~/Unix_work/Misc/ to a file called home_list.txt.

7.3.3 Combining Commands

Entering individual command lines becomes tedious, especially when you wish to perform a sequence of tasks. To combat this tedium, shells provide many different options for combining command lines. For instance, you can separate independent command lines with the semicolon (;):

STEP 66: ENTER MULTIPLE COMMANDS IN SEQUENCE

```
dis% cd ~/Unix_work; pwd        Change to Unix-work directory; and then, check CWD.

/home/dis/Unix_work             Both commands worked in succession: first cd and then pwd.
```

Pipes provide other useful connectors. Pipes cause results of one command to act upon another command. Pipes use the symbol bar (|). The standard syntax for *piping* two commands is ***command1* | *command2***. Output from the first command line is acted upon by the second. As an example, try listing everything in your entire system by piping the *recursive listing,* **ls -R**, to the **more** command. The option, **-R**, causes **ls** to list directories and all subsequent subdirectories:

STEP 67: PIPING TWO COMMANDS TOGETHER

```
dis% ls -R /   List everything starting from root. You should hit ^C really soon to stop this madness.

Thousands of files will fly down your monitor or window.

dis% ls -R / | more               Now, look at everything in your entire Unix tree in
                                   more leisurely fashion. more will view the output of ls -R /.

Press the Spacebar to look at these hundreds of files. Press q to quit at some point.
```

Your shell interprets the command line **ls -R / | more** as "pipe the output of **ls -R** into the command **more**."

PRACTICE!

> **6.** In the same command line, change your CWD to HOME and display HOME's contents.
>
> **7.** Display the entire contents of your HOME directory. (Be sure to page through the output.)
>
> **8.** What is the difference between **ls > ~/list.txt ; more list.txt** and **ls | more**? Which command line do you prefer?

7.4 FINDING COMMANDS

The commands in this text will suffice for general Unix usage. However, sooner or later you will need a more obscure command to complete other tasks. Yes, command options abound, and you'll never memorize all of them. This section shows where to find and locate other commands.

7.4.1 Everything Is a File

State aloud and repeat this mantra: *Unix treats everything as a file*.

How is this true? Remember, *everything* in the directory tree has a pathname. All commands, all devices, all files, and all directories have names and locations. Pretend that each item is a file, each with its various contents. For instance, command-files contain instructions that, when activated, cause the program to run.

7.4.2 Programming

How are programs created? A programmer writes code, a series of instructions usually written in a computer language with ASCII text. Compiling the program typically converts the instructions into binary form, a sequence of "1"s and "0"s called bits. In fact, programs stored in binary files are often called *binaries*. Compiled programs are typically unintelligible to all but operating systems.

7.4.3 Executing Commands

Executing and *running* programs both refer to activating and using software. Often, entering a program name activates and runs the program. Many Unix tools are invoked by simply entering *pathname*. Several of the commands you have used, in fact, are programs. However, specifying full pathnames is not always necessary, as discussed below.

How do you know which files are programs? Use **ls -F** to show file types. Files shown with an asterisk (*), such as *filename**, are called **executables**, programs that you can run. In general, system commands are executables.

7.4.4 Where Are the Commands?

Unix executables are usually binary files or shell scripts. Binary files include compiled programs as discussed above. Shell scripts, programs written in shell programming languages, provide customized Unix tools. (Chapter 8 provides a small taste of shell languages.) Due to customized configurations, each Unix system directory stores programs in different locations. However, many directories share similar organizational structures.

Binary (bin) directories store many executables. Common directories such as /bin/, /usr/bin/, /util/bin/, /usr/local/bin/, and others categorize commands by different criteria. Many systems also contain alternate Unix-versions of commands. For instance, does your system support a Berkeley Software Distribution (BSD) directory, /usr/ucb/bin/ or /bsd/bin/? For common SVR4 commands, try looking inside a common bin directory:

<table>
<tr><td rowspan="4">STEP 68:
LOOKING
INSIDE A
SYSTEM
DIRECTORY</td><td><code>dis% cd /usr/bin/</code></td><td>Change your CWD to a directory that contains system programs.</td></tr>
<tr><td><code>dis% ls -F | more</code></td><td>Investigate the contents. Asterisks (*) indicate binaries.</td></tr>
<tr><td colspan="2">You will see a rather lengthy listing. See other "bin" directories as well.</td></tr>
</table>

You should see a variety of command name binaries inside /usr/bin/.

7.4.5 PATH Variables

While interpreting command lines, shells must ensure that each command exists on your system. Shells already "know" certain commands built into the shell called "shell builtins". Your PATH variable helps your shell find other commands in system directories. This sequence of directories, *dir1:dir2:...*, separated by colons (:) comprises the PATH variable. Look inside one of your system configuration files such as .cshrc or .kshrc to find PATH. You can also use **echo** to display your current PATH:

<table>
<tr><td rowspan="3">STEP 69:
CHECKING
PATH VARIABLE</td><td><code>dis% echo $PATH</code></td><td>Display the directories that your shell searches when looking for commands.</td></tr>
<tr><td><code>/usr/bin:/util/bin:/usr/ucb:/util/gnu/bin</code></td><td>Your path might look different.</td></tr>
<tr><td></td><td>Colons (:) separate the directories that your shell searches.</td></tr>
</table>

You can modify your PATH to include more directories in which to search. Just append another directory path preceded by a colon. Note that C Shells typically denote PATH in lowercase letters.

7.4.6 Locating Commands

If you cannot execute a certain command, add that command's directory to your PATH. Before adding directories, though, first check if the command's directory already belongs to PATH. Enter **type** *command* to discover the location of *command*. For instance, determine the location of **exit** and **mailx**:

<table>
<tr><td rowspan="4">STEP 70:
DETERMINE
LOCATION OF
COMMANDS</td><td><code>dis% type exit</code></td><td>Where is the command exit?</td></tr>
<tr><td><code>exit is a shell builtin</code></td><td>Yes, shells provide the command exit.</td></tr>
<tr><td><code>dis% type mailx</code></td><td>Where is the command mailx?</td></tr>
<tr><td><code>mailx is /usr/bin/mailx</code></td><td>mailx is stored in /usr/bin/.</td></tr>
</table>

If **type** can indeed find a command that will not execute, check with a system administrator on the command's use if trouble persists. The command line **man shell_builtins** provides a complete listing of shell builtins. (**man** is discussed in the next section.) Some systems duplicate builtins in other `bin` directories. C Shell users should try **which command** to determine locations. Korn Shell users can use **whence -p command** instead for the same purpose.

7.4.7 Activating Commands

When using a command "unknown" to your shell, simply enter **pathname** to activate the command. After locating the command, enter the absolute pathname followed by options and arguments:

<table>
<tr><td style="vertical-align:top; text-align:right; font-weight:bold">STEP 71:
DIRECT
ACTIVATION OF
COMMANDS</td><td>

```
dis% type lpq
```
Where is the command lpq?

```
lpq is /usr/ucb/lpq
```
lpq is a BSD command that shows printer queues.
If not available, try type ls to demonstrate.

```
dis% /usr/ucb/lpq
```
Activate lpq. Be sure to use your system's path.

```
no entries
```
lpq shows a list of pending print jobs.

</td></tr>
</table>

You should add frequently used "unknown" system directories to PATH to save time in typing.

PRACTICE!

9. What is the pathname of the binary **mv**? Try **which** if you run a C Shell.
10. List the pathname of **mv** with **ls -F**. Why is an asterisk (*) appended to **mv**?
11. What are two methods of activating **pwd**?
12. Why would you get an error message for entering the command line, **/home/~username/Unix_work/**?

7.5 ON-LINE HELP

Does your system have **help** or **learn** installed? If so, these programs provide good tutorials and quick instruction. Most Unix systems provide on-line help for investigating commands via ***manual pages***, which are on-line documents that describe system commands and command options. Enter **man command** to find help on **command**. (See also **xman** for a GUI version of manual pages.)

While accessing one may be a snap, *deciphering* a manual page is another matter entirely. The trick is to ignore all of the complex, unnecessary information—focus on command syntax, description, and options.

First, use **man** to learn about **man**:

<table>
<tr><td style="vertical-align:top; text-align:right; font-weight:bold">STEP 72:
MANUAL PAGE
PORTION</td><td>

```
dis% man man
```
Find manual page on man.

```
man(1)          User Commands          man(1)
```
Manual page title.

```
NAME
```
Command name and description.

```
    man - find and display reference manual pages
```

</td></tr>
</table>

```
SYNOPSIS                        Basic command syntax. Sometimes many variations are available.
      man [ - ] [ -adFlrt ] [ -M path ] [ -T macro-package ]
            [-s section ] name ...
      man [ -M path ] -k keyword ...
      man [ -M path ] -f file ...
```

More sections follow. Usually, manual pages are piped through **more**.
Otherwise, enter **man man|more** *next time.*

When reading this and other manual pages, remember the general Unix syntax, ***command options arguments***. On this page, the text [-adFlrt] indicates options acceptable for use with **man**. For instance, **man -a command** forms an acceptable command line. (Never type the brackets!) The text [-M path] indicates that the **-M** option requires a pathname for an argument. Scrolling further down the page will reveal full descriptions of all command options.

Manual pages include more portions than illustrated here: DESCRIPTION provides a longer description of the command. All possible options shown in SYNOPSIS are described in detail in the OPTIONS section. Sometimes the EXAMPLES section demonstrates common usage. Other sections, such as LOCATION and VARIABLES, help customize the command. Find other manual pages on commands listed in SEE ALSO for further study.

The manual pages are organized into several sections, often divided into categories numbered from 1 to 9. Here, the title man(1) indicates that you have accessed section 1 of the manual pages directory. Other commands are located in different sections. Sometimes commands even have different versions and may be found in more than one section. Common commands are stored in sections 1 and 2. Try **man -a command** to see *all* manual pages associated with **command**. Use **man -s section command** to access a particular section. (In a GUI environment, **xman** provides a good menu listing of sections.)

PRACTICE!

13. Look up the manual page for **ls**.
14. What option tells **ls** to sort output across the screen instead of down?
15. What does the command line **man -k browse** do?
16. Many manual pages summarize available commands on intro pages. Try loading the intro page for manual section 3.

7.6 PROCESS MANAGEMENT

Every program consumes computer memory, and engineering and science programs consume plenty! Be considerate of others on your network, especially when running memory-hogging software. How to manage your programs and memory usage is discussed in this section.

7.6.1 Processes

Each program that you execute and run is called a ***process***, or a ***job***. From logging in to logging out, processes encompass nearly everything you activate. Basic tasks such as routine file management consume very little resources, while big software applications can eat up large portions of memory.

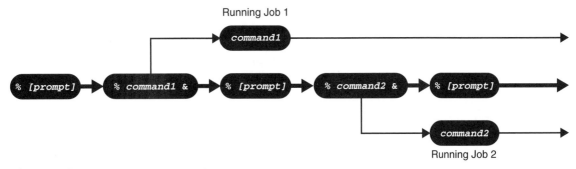

Figure 7.3. Multiprocessing as "Forking"

7.6.2 Multiprocessing

Simultaneously running several programs is called ***multiprocessing*** or *multitasking*. GUIs provide a good example of multiprocessing. Different windows and utilities appear on your screen, running continuously even while you perform other tasks.

Conceptualize multiprocessing as the ***forking*** illustrated in Figure 7.3. Processes "fork" each time a new process is activated while another still runs. Your main command line, the *parent* process, spawns *child* processes. Each child process begins when you activate commands and programs at the prompt. In Figure 7.3, the prompt indicates the parent process, the middle "prong" (*tine*) on the fork. Commands 1 and 2 activate new child processes: Jobs 1 and 2. These child processes fork off of the parent, running separately and simultaneously with each other and their parent. In fact, all of the commands performed in a Unix session generate child processes of the shell.

7.6.3 Process Listing

When you run multiple processes simultaneously, you might lose track of them all. Monitor your jobs with **ps**, the *process status* command. **ps** will list jobs running on the system and information about these jobs. The information includes the processes' unique process ID number (PID), your terminal location (TTY), process duration (TIME), and command, or program, name (CMD).

STEP 73: REPORT CURRENT PROCESSES	
dis% **ps**	*Report your "major" (parent) processes.*
PID TTY TIME CMD	*Process information for Dave. Yours will look different.*
4654 pts/2 0:03 csh	*Notice how your shell is a process.*
4755 pts/2 8:27 maker5X.	*See my word processor? Book writing takes a long time!*

Without options, **ps** displays only "major" or parent processes, programs without subsequent child processes. Enter **ps -f** to obtain *fuller* detail on your major processes such as full pathnames. View all of your processes with **ps -fu *username***. To see *every* process running on your network, enter **ps -e**, a potentially gigantic listing. Enter **ps -fe** for a full listing of every process (some systems also support the BSD version of this command, **ps -aux**).

7.6.4 Suspending a Process

What happens if you enter a wrong command? Or, perhaps the system hangs and you just can't stick around? First, try to kill the process with **^C**. ***Killing*** a process means interrupting and eradicating the job. If killing fails, then try ***suspending*** the process with **^Z**. Suspending tells Unix to only interrupt the process. Unix returns your prompt. You can then leave the job on hold, restart it, or destroy it.

Try suspending and killing. Start a process with **cat**. Edit a file called ben.txt. Then, suspend the process with **^Z**:

STEP 74: **SUSPEND** **PROCESS**	`dis% cd`	*Return to HOME directory.*
	`dis% cat > ben.txt`	*Create a file called* ben.txt *using* **cat**.
	Control-Z will suspend a process. **^Z**	*Start editing* ben.txt. *Type this sentence.* *Press* **^Z** *to suspend the* **cat** *process.*
	`dis% ps`	*The prompt reappears. Check process listing. Also, try* **ps -o pid,s,comm**.
	`PID  TTY      TIME CMD`	*Process information for Dave. Yours will look different.*
	`4654 pts/2    0:03 csh`	*This process is still running.*
	`4755 pts/2    8:27 maker5X.`	*This process is still running.*
	`5216 pts/2    0:00 cat`	*This is the process corresponding to* **cat > ben.txt**.

To display process states, enter **ps -o pid,s,comm** for the PID, state, and command name of your major processes. A "T" in the "S" column indicates a suspended process. The process **cat > ben.txt** is now pending. The job awaits your decision....

7.6.5 Killing a Process

Suppose that you wish to stop editing **ben.txt**, that is, to destroy the suspended process. To kill **cat > ben.txt**, use **kill *PID***. ("PID", the process identification number, was displayed in Step 74.)

STEP 75: **KILL PROCESS**	`dis% kill 5216`	*Destroy the* **cat > ben.txt** *process.*
	`dis% ps`	*Check the process listing. You should not see* **cat** *listed.*
	`PID  TTY      TIME CMD`	*Process information for Dave. Yours will look different.*
	`4654 pts/2    0:03 csh`	*This process is still running.*
	`4755 pts/2    8:27 maker5X.`	*This process is still running.*
	`[1] + Terminated  cat > ben.txt 5216 pts/2`	**cat > ben.txt** *is now killed,* *vaporized from the system.*

Because suspending processes involves memory usage, you should first try **^C** (kill) to terminate a running process. When **^C** fails, follow the sequence: **^Z**, **ps**, **kill *PID***. That is, suspend, find PID, and kill the process.

Sometimes remnants of the original command ("zombies") persist after termination. If zombies linger in your process listing after a kill action, use **kill -9 *PID*** to utterly obliterate all remaining traces of the offending process. (Unix can be quite gruesome!)

One last tip: avoid killing your shell process: unless you have multiple windows open, you will log yourself out! GUI applications have menu options to close or destroy individual windows.

7.6.6 Background

As discussed previously, a number of processes run simultaneously, or fork off the shell, in any Unix session. Display, for instance, a full process listing of your present session with **ps -fu** *username*. Though you may see nothing but a prompt, there's a lot going on. All those other processes run in the ***background***. Background jobs continue working without command-line input, happily running elsewhere—in other memory locations—while you continue to work on the task at hand. Thus, background processes leave your Unix prompt free to accept more commands.

Appending an ampersand (&) to a command line pushes that process into the background. Be sure to place the ampersand at the end on the command line. See how this works by creating a list of system users, while continuing to work:

**STEP 76:
BACKGROUND
PROCESSES**

```
dis% listusers > lu.txt &
```
Generate a text file of a list of system accounts.
Use **finger david** *if* **listusers** *is not available.*

```
dis% pwd
```
Your prompt returns. Now, continue working on something else.

```
/home/dis
[1]   Done              listusers > lu.txt
```
Here is output from **pwd**.
Unix reports that the other job is done.

```
dis%
```
Your prompt is ready for more action.

```
dis% more lu.txt
```
View the results of your work.

While you were running other commands, Unix created lu.txt. The job, **listusers > lu.txt**, ran in the background as illustrated in Figure 7.4. See also Figure 7.3.

GUIs provide a good model of background processes. In a GUI, different windows perform different, all simultaneously, each with their own command prompts accepting separate command lines. When running GUI programs, enter commands as ***command &*** to free up terminal windows for further command entry.

7.6.7 Foreground

If not sent to the background with the ampersand, your commands run in the ***foreground***. The main forks shown in Figures 7.3 and 7.4, the parents, constitute foregrounds. Unix sequentially processes foreground commands at the command prompt. Therefore, new command lines must wait for old commands to finish executing before new commands can be entered.

Figure 7.4.   Running a Process in the Background

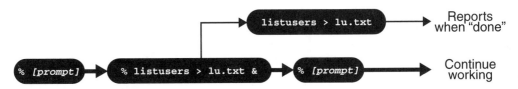

7.6.8 Job Shell

Job shells provide further means to manage your background processes, enabling you to run, suspend, restart, or destroy as you need to. Enter **jobs** to provide a numbered list of background and suspended processes. Note the numbers. Like PIDs provided by the **ps** command, job numbers help you access your jobs in the job shell.

Suppose that you start a process and suspend it with **^Z**. Now, you want to reestablish the process. First, find the number and status of this suspended process from **jobs**. Then, select one of the following process management steps:

- Run the job in *foreground*: Enter **fg %*jobnumber***, or just **%*jobnumber***
- Restart the job in *background*: Enter **bg %*jobnumber***
- *Suspend* the job: Enter **stop %*jobnumber***
- *Destroy* the job: Enter **kill %*jobnumber***

Now, practice managing a job via the job shell:

STEP 77:
JOB SHELL

dis% **cat > nvp.txt &**	*Send editing of* nvp.txt *to the background.*
dis% **jobs**	*List current background and suspended jobs.*
[1] + Suspended (tty input) cat > nvp.txt	*"1" is the job number, or label.*
	*Some versions might say "*stopped*".*
dis% **fg %1**	*Bring* **cat > nvp.txt**, *job* 1, *to the foreground.*
cat > nvp.txt	*Unix tells you that job* 1 *is back in business.*
Start typing this line.	*You can now recommence editing.*
^Z	*Suspend the process again by pressing* **^Z**.
dis% **kill %1**	*Now, kill the process.*

Use **jobs** *when available. Otherwise, you will need* **ps -o pid,s,comm**, *a rather inconvenient command, to show process states.*

PRACTICE!

Read each step of the following exercise before starting. You might have to type the commands rather quickly.

17. Place the process **finger ira > ira.txt** in the background.
18. Show your process and job listings.
19. Bring **finger ira > ira.txt** to the foreground.
20. Suspend, and kill the process using the job number. Did Unix finish the process before you killed the job?

7.7 APPLICATION: COMPILING AND RUNNING PROGRAMS

In this section, you will compile your hello.C program.

7.7.1 Problem

Before submitting your work to your client, you ought to actually test your code. Does your program perform as the client requested?

7.7.2 Background

To activate the program, compile the code into executable files. Unix typically supports the C compiler, **cc**, and the FORTRAN 77 compiler, **f77**. Beware, however, that not all versions of Unix support the same compiling programs. Also, inspect GNU compilers such as **gcc** and **g++**, if available. Eventually, you should investigate files called Makefile to more effectively compile larger programs.

7.7.3 Methodology

You need to locate, understand, and use the compiler. Either check with your system administrator for literature or venture forth with **man** pages. When compiling the program, your compiler might complain of errors—be sure to enter the code from Chapter 3 exactly as shown.

7.7.4 Solution

Many tools explored in this chapter will assist your work. Judicious use of **man** pages helps:

STEP 78: **SEARCH FOR** **C++ MANUAL** **PAGES**	`dis% `**`man -k C++`**	*Do a keyword search for manual pages discussing* `C++`.

```
CC   CC   (1)        - C++ compilation system
g++  g++  (1)        - GNU project C++ Compiler
g++  gcc  (1)        - GNU project C and C++ Compiler (v2.7)
gcc  gcc  (1)        - GNU project C and C++ Compiler (v2.7)
```
Try this compiler for your C++ program. Note the uppercase "C".

You might see many more suggested items as well.

`dis% `**`man -s1 CC | more`** *`CC(1)` indicates the CC manual page is located in section 1 (**s1**). Read the C++ manual page. Your compiler might be different. There will be a blizzard of options; Review **-o** and **-help** in particular.*

To create an executable file using the CC compiler, enter **CC -o** *executable-filename filename*, which will create an executable file that activates your program:

STEP 79: **COMPILE AND** **EXECUTE YOUR** **PROGRAM**	`dis% `**`cd ~/PROJECTS/Hello/`**	*Change your CWD to your* `Hello/` *subdirectory.*

`dis% `**`CC -o HELLO hello.C`** *Compile your* `hello.C` *program. Also, create an executable file called* **HELLO** *with the* **-o** *option*

You may receive compiler warnings. If so, check your file for errors. Then, try compiling again.

`dis% `**`HELLO`** *Run your program. When* **cc** *finishes, the prompt will appear.*

`Hello World!` *Congratulations! Your program properly executed.*

`dis%` *Your Unix prompt returns.*

You can also redirect output from your program as with other Unix commands:

<table>
<tr><td rowspan="6">STEP 80:
REDIRECT
OUTPUT FROM A
PROGRAM</td><td><code>dis% HELLO > hello.out</code></td><td>Redirect output from your HELLO program to <code>hello.out</code>.</td></tr>
<tr><td><code>dis% ls -aF</code></td><td>List all files with types inside the CWD.</td></tr>
<tr><td><code>./ ../ HELLO* hello.C hello.out</code></td><td>Here are your files.
The * signifies an executable file.</td></tr>
<tr><td><code>dis% more hello.out</code></td><td>View the contents of your redirected output.</td></tr>
<tr><td><code>Hello World!</code></td><td>Your program stored the output inside <code>hello.out</code>.</td></tr>
<tr><td><code>dis% mailx boss</code></td><td>Report your success. Maybe Stuart will give you that well-deserved raise!</td></tr>
</table>

In the next chapter, you will set permissions such that others can view and execute your work.

CHAPTER SUMMARY

This chapter explored a variety of Unix tools in depth. Many programs and software operations are bundled with the operating system. Most tools can be organized in general categories. Among the most important of programs is the shell. Shells interpret command lines and provide methods for redirecting input and output. You explored other tools using manual pages, which are on-line Unix documentation. Finally, process management was introduced to help you more efficiently perform your work.

KEY TERMS

background	job	process
executable	killing	redirection
foreground	manual page	standard I/O
forking	multiprocessing	suspending
Input/Output (I/O)	pipe	tools

APPLICATION: HOW TO TAKE A COMPUTER-ORIENTED TEST

Have you done as well as you expected on your tests? Do you experience test anxiety? If so, does the anxiety occur before or after the test? Or, perhaps at both times? In any case, stop! Take a deep breath and pause for moment....

Instructors give tests, in part, to motivate study. Honestly, many students would skip studying if reproducing material were not mandatory. Also, tests measure and compare student performance, and unfortunately, this produces internal and external pressures on students to succeed, all of which only agitates students. Nevertheless, you *can* alleviate test anxiety.

Computer tests are tricky and come in many forms. Whatever the case, never even think about cramming for a computer-based test. Using software involves skill, and skill *always* requires practice. To study, sit in front of a computer with this book. Check each command and step; train with practice and homework problems. Obtain solutions to your homework after you've submitted your assignment. Seek help when you become stuck. Do additional problems from this book and others as well.

Start studying *at least* one week before your test. If you have the time, create study sheets that combine and summarize lecture notes, homework, and the text. Writing your own notes drums material into your mind and helps breaks the tedium of reading. (And from just finishing them, you will gain sense of accomplishment as well.) Sometimes classes even permit "cheat sheets" during tests, and concocting great cheat sheets yields terrific comprehension. When developing study sheets, write a list of all commands and options, always note syntax, and show how options affect each command. Give examples that demonstrate command usage.

Be advised that engineering and science tests require you to *apply* your knowledge. Can you use your acquired knowledge to solve problems and draw conclusions? Yes, sometimes teachers test material that

you have never seen, but you will be ready to handle this if you know not only *what,* but *how* and *why* as well. So, first memorize the *what,* basic commands and syntax as a safety precaution—memorization typically produces passing grades at a minimum. Next, study the *how* and *why* for a better grade. Finally, practice applying this knowledge to example problems for an even better grade.

If you *still* perform badly, pick yourself off the ground, shake off the dust, and try again. Everyone has bad days. Understanding the material is more important in the long run. You will do better next time. Success is not always doing well: success is also fighting in the face of defeat. Never give up! A bit more effort will give you the world.

Problems

1. What is a Unix tool?
2. List five categories of Unix tools.
3. What is a shell? Describe some tasks that a shell performs.
4. Will your shell permit **lp** *-file dprinter*? Will this command line work?
5. Is the command line **lp -wd** *printer file* acceptable? If so, what does this command line do?
6. Is the command line **who am i** the same as **who -am -i**? Why or why not?
7. Can you use **-F** with **ls** such that the option comes *after* the directory? For example, is **ls /home/dis/ -F** an acceptable command line?
8. How you do list all contents of a directory without displaying the current working directory (.) and its parent (. .)?
9. What is the difference between the command lines **ls -R > list.txt** and **ls -R | more** ?
10. Show the command line for printing out a listing of your HOME directory by piping output to a printer.
11. What is the pathname of the command **telnet**?
12. Why should the command line for mailing someone a file, **mailx** *username* **<** *file*, use the "**<**" operator?
13. How can you append a sequence of text files together? (Hint: What is the definition of *concatenate*?) Show a command line for appending the files f1.txt and f2.txt together in a new file, t3.txt.
14. How might you use **cat** with input and output redirection to first create and then copy a text file?
15. How do you remove a filename that starts with a dash (-)?
16. How do you remove a filename that includes a blank space? (Hint: Find your shell manual page.)
17. What is the difference between *killing* and *suspending* a process?

18. What are three ways of killing a process? What are two ways of suspending a process? (Sorry, using a GUI command does not count.)

19. Assuming that you are using a GUI, how would activate **xman** from a command line such that your prompt returns? Is **xman** running in the foreground or background?

20. Describe the series of steps that you would take to use the job shell to place two processes in the background.

21. Project 1: List and describe ten different shell builtin-commands.

22. Project 2: Draw analogies between file management and process management. Discuss parallels between parent-child relationships. Relate similarities and differences. Be sure to include several examples. Edit your report with a text editor.

8

Advanced Unix

8.1 UNIX ALTERNATIVES

Unix owes its enduring popularity to the power and elegance Unix offers. Many large institutions employ Unix. The personal-computer user can also install Unix. Programmers from around the world provide cheap and exciting Unix alternatives, such as GNU and Linux.

8.1.1 GNU

Besides commercial versions of Unix, many systems have installed **GNU**, a collection of utilities offered by the Free Software Foundation. Many of GNU ("Gnu's Not Unix") programs have the look and feel of Unix, but offer added functionality and efficiency. One GNU application, **emacs**, is a tremendously powerful text editor enhanced with several useful features. (See Appendix C.) GNU even comes equipped with its own manual pages. Look inside your system's util/ or usr/ directories for gnu/. You should also consult with your system administrators about GNU's availability.

8.1.2 Linux

In 1991, a student at the University of Helsinki, Linus Torvalds, developed his own Unix-like kernel, an operating system "core", called **Linux**. Much of Linux borrows GNU software such as **bash**, and all source code is freely available. Programmers from around the world continually volunteer time to improving the code and broadening Linux's capabilities. Many consider Linux a cheap, powerful, and functional alternative to other operating systems, especially for personal-computer users.

OBJECTIVES

After reading this chapter, you should be able to:

- Grasp advanced Unix topics
- Assign file access permissions
- Manage account usage
- Understand shell customizing and command aliases

8.2 TEXT OPERATIONS

Before the advent of WYSIWYG ("What You See Is What You Get") editors, people relied on Unix tools for many text file operations. Even today, many utilities, such as those in Table 8-1, are quite handy. Use **man** to thoroughly investigate these commands. Try, for instance, searching for a text pattern inside a group of files contained in your Unix_work/ subdirectory with **grep**:

STEP 81: SEARCH FOR PATTERNS IN FILES

dis% **cd ~/Unix_work/**   *Work inside your* Unix_work/ *directory.*

Now, create two text files in which to search for text. Use **cat** *as a quick text editor.*
dis% **cat > test1.txt**   *Create a text file,* test1.txt.
Hello, Unix is fun!   *Add this line.*
This is another line.   *Add this line.*
^D   *Exit.*

dis% **cat > test2.txt**   *Create a text file,* test2.txt.
Hello, Unix is fun!   *Add this line.*
This is an uninteresting line.   *Add this line.*
Hello, Unix is fun!   *Add this line.*
^D   *Exit.*

dis% **grep -n 'Unix is fun!' test1.txt test2.txt**   *Look for the pattern,*
*"*Unix is fun!*", inside indicated text files. The "*-n*" option will indicate the line number where* **grep** *finds the pattern. Also, try entering* **grep 'Unix is fun!' *** *to save time (See Section 8.5 for the wildcard *).*

test1.txt:1:Unix is fun!   *Unix reports each instance of the pattern.*
test2.txt:1:Unix is fun!   *Unix also reports the line number inside the file.*
test2.txt:3:Unix is fun!   *Unix reports multiple occurences as well.*

Sometimes these patterns are called *strings*. Usually, surround longer patterns with single (**' '**) or double (**" "**) quotes, especially when searching for characters other than numbers and letters.

PRACTICE!

1. Create a banner out of your username. Store the banner in a file called me.txt.
2. Check the spelling in your test1.txt file with Unix.

8.3 FILE SECURITY

After awhile, your account may contain hundreds of separate files, and you might want to protect them from others' eyes for a variety of reasons.

8.3.1 Security and Privacy
Thus far, you have changed your current working directory with relative ease. Users, however, cannot necessarily freely traverse the Unix directory tree. Due to privacy and security concerns, Unix prevents unwanted snooping. Also, just imagine if you could accidentally delete root! Sometimes, though, you must grant, or be granted, access for sharing data in normally inaccessible places. Other users, for example, might require data, programs, and information pertaining to group projects.

TABLE 8-1 Common Text-File Operations

COMMAND	SYNTAX	DESCRIPTION
banner	banner *pattern*	Displays a gigantic ASCII image of **pattern**. Try **banner IRA > ira.txt**.
comm	comm *options file1 file2*	Compare the contents of **file1** with **file2**. Produces three columns: lines in **file1**, lines in **file2**, lines in both.
diff	diff *options file1 file2*	Report differences between two text files.
dircmp	dircmp *options dir1 dir2*	Compare contents of two directories.
find	find *pathnames conditions*	Find files or directories. Try these options. **-print**: print results to screen (mandatory if you want to see the results); **-name**: provide name of file; and **-user**: files belonging to **user**.
grep	grep *options pattern files*	Find a pattern in a file or group of files. Use double-quotes when the pattern has blank spaces (" "), and a star (*) for *all* files in CWD: **grep "text string" ***.
head	head *options file*	View the top, or beginning, of a file.
sort	sort *options file*	Sort file contents (alphabetical-review options for other schemes).
spell	spell *options file*	Check the spelling in a text file's contents.
split	split *options file1 file2*	Split text files into smaller ones.
tail	tail *options file*	View the bottom, or end, of a text file.
uniq	uniq *options file1 file2*	Remove duplicate lines from a file. You might wish to first use **sort**.
wc	wc *options file*	Count items such as words and lines. (Also, try **cat -n** for numbering lines.)

8.3.2 Ownership and Permission

Consider each user as an owner. You own the files that you create and store in your account. Thus, Unix automatically provides you with permission to access, view, or modify your own files and directories. Outside of your account, Unix does not necessarily grant you the same permissions. Only system administrators have complete access to the entire system. Don't worry! They will not pry into your account unless absolutely necessary.

8.3.3 Long Listing

How do you determine ownership and permissions of directory contents? Try listing directory contents in *long format* with **ls -l**:

STEP 82:
LONG LISTING

```
dis% ls -l ~        List in long format the content of HOME. Be sure to use a lowercase letter L!

This is a portion of the listing:
drwx------   2  dis   ciegrad   512     Sep 21 20:00   Unix_work
-rw-r-----   1  dis   ciegrad   16490   Sep 24 21:12   test1.txt
    ①        ②   ③      ④        ⑤         ⑥     ⑦         ⑧
```

From left to right, the long list shows eight fields: ① file type and permissions (discussed in next section), ② links (skip this), ③ owner, ④ group, ⑤ size in bytes, ⑥ last modification date, ⑦ last modification time, and ⑧ the name.

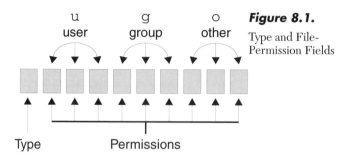

Figure 8.1.

Type and File-Permission Fields

In this example, the fields for `Unix_work/` describe a 512-byte directory that was last modified on September 21 at 8 P.M. The directory is owned by user `dis`, who belongs to `ciegrad`, a *group*. A group is a collection of users with common identification. Enter **groups** to display the groups to which you belong. Try combining **ls -l** with **-a** as **ls -al** for a total listing in long format.

8.3.4 File Permissions

All items in the directory have ***file permissions*** that determine who can read, write, and execute the files. For instance, you, the owner, have permission to copy and delete your own files.

The first ten characters in the long listing indicate first the file type and then, nine permissions. Look at Step 82, item ①. `Unix_work/` has the type and permission fields `drwx------`. Think of these ten fields as *slots,* as shown in Figure 8.1. Each slot must be filled. Starting from the left, the first slot contains `d` or `-`. The `d` here indicates that Unix work is a directory. A dash (`-`) indicates a file. (Unix provides further file types: enter **man ls** for a complete description.)

The next nine slots show file permissions. These slots divide into three sets of three slots: The first three slots correspond to owner, or *user*, permission; the second three slots show permissions for the user's *group*; and the final three slots indicate permissions for the world, or *other*. Unix abbreviates user, group, and other fields as u, g, and o.

One of four characters can fill each permission slot: a dash (`-`) indicates no permission given; `r` grants read permissions, such as copying and directory listing; `w` allows writing permissions such as adding to, creating, and deleting files; and `x` provides execute permission. (See Table 8-2.)

TABLE 8-2   File and Directory Permissions

	SYMBOL MEANING	FILE PERMISSIONS GRANTED	DIRECTORY PERMISSIONS GRANTED
–	*None*	none	none
r	*Read*	view contents	list contents
w	*Write*	edit, delete	modify, add, or remove files
x	*Execute*	execute a program	enter (access) a directory

Each of the three slots in the user, group, and other fields corresponds to a level of permissions, and is filled with the appropriate letter or a dash. The first slot shows read permission, the second shows write permission, and the third shows execute permission. The dash *removes* permission for the given field.

Now considering these rules, `drwx--x--x`, for example, indicates a *directory* with all *user* permissions, but only *execute* permission for *group* and *other*. So, the user can

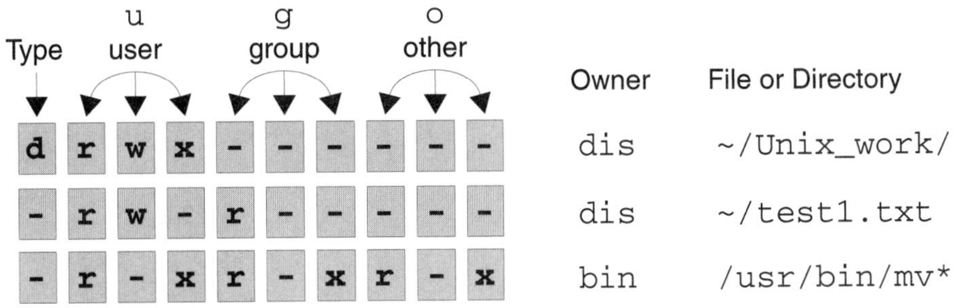

Figure 8.2. Example File Permissions

read, write, and execute, but anyone else may only execute (access) this directory. Totally restricting permissions on a directory yields d---------, while allowing total directory access for everyone would yield drwxrwxrwx. Figure 8.2 shows further examples.

Investigate the permissions for the system command **mv**:

STEP 83:
LISTING FILE
PERMISSIONS

```
dis% ls -l /usr/bin/mv                    Long list the system command mv.
                              Enter type mv if you are uncertain of the directory.

-r-xr-xr-x  1  bin  bin  16644  May 2 1996  /usr/bin/mv
```

Recall how **mv** is called a binary, or executable. Thus, **mv** grants execute permission to everyone. Although everyone also has *read* permission as well, the system administrators removed *write* permission. The program is thus safe from unscrupulous or accidental deletion.

PRACTICE!

Consider the example permissions from Steps 82 and 83 and Figure 8.2.

3. What are file permissions for ~/Unix_work/?

4. What are the file permissions for ~/test1.txt?

5. What file permissions on HOME will allow users to access ~/test1.txt?

6. Why can the file permissions for **/usr/bin/mv*** *not* be listed as drrxrrxrrx?

8.3.5 Changing Permissions

The command **chmod**, *change mode,* sets file permissions. Using **chmod**, the owner of a file or directory can add or subtract read, write, and execute permissions to the user, group, or other fields. The syntax for **chmod** is **chmod *users + or - permissions pathname***. Follow these instructions to change file permissions:

- Choose any combination of ***users*** from **u**, **g**, or **o**, such as **ug** or **go**. To change permissions for all three you may use **a** (*all*) in place of **ugo**.
- Use the plus sign (**+**) to add permissions to slots or minus sign (**-**) to subtract permissions from slots.
- Choose the ***permissions*** you wish to change from combinations of **r**, **w**, and **x**.
- Identify a file or directory for ***pathname***.

Suppose user `klezb` enters **chmod go-x /home/klezb/**: this command line removes group and other access permissions on `klezb`'s HOME. `klezb`'s HOME is now safe from prying eyes.

Try adding only access permission to your HOME for everyone:

**STEP 84:
CHANGING
PERMISSIONS**

dis% **cd**	*Change CWD to HOME.*
dis% **cd ../**	*Change CWD to parent directory of HOME.*
	(You could also change to HOME with **cd /home/** *or the more interesting* **cd ~/../**.*)*
dis% **chmod a+x dis/**	*Change permissions on your own HOME directory.*
	Group and other will now have permission to enter your HOME.
dis% **chmod go-rw dis/**	*Remove read and write permissions on your HOME for group and other.*
dis% **ls -l | more**	*Look at everyone's accounts. Pipe the output through* **more**.

Some other users...
```
drwx--x--x  27  dis  ciegrad  2560  Nov 1 01:02  dis        See the x's?
```
Some other users...

chmod a+x *username* tells Unix to change the permission on *username*: for all users (**a**), you are adding (**+**) execute (**x**) permission. "Execute" permission on a directory means that people can access, but not necessarily list—listing requires r permissions. (Adding only x is a special Unix trick. Users can access pathnames only if they know the names.)

File permissions can create havoc if misused. Never add write permission for group or other, and be careful with read permissions. Certainly, do not subtract any user permission on your own HOME directory! If you tire from changing permissions for files one at a time, investigate **umask**. **umask** sets default permissions on files newly created in each session. Also, review manual pages on both **chmod** and **umask** for an alternate, numerical method of assigning permissions.

PRACTICE!

7. Do you have group and other permissions set for reading or writing on your HOME directory? How do you check?

8. What is the command for removing group and other reading permission on your account? Enter the command if these permissions exist.

9. Modify your account such that everyone can access and list only your `~/Unix_work/` subdirectory. Do not let anyone, save yourself, list your HOME. Be sure to double check with a long listing.

8.4 FILE MANAGEMENT

This section reviews advanced topics in managing your account.

8.4.1 Renaming and Moving Entire Directories

Moving and deleting individual files quickly becomes tedious—imagine having to remove directories with hundreds or perhaps thousands of files. To save users from this agony, Unix provides commands for reorganizing directories as well as files. Use **cp -r** *oldpath* *newpath* to copy an entire directory along with its contents and **mv** *oldpath* *newpath* to move a directory with its contents. Also, consult **man ln** for links.

8.4.2 Deleting Files and Directories

A directory with any contents at all cannot be deleted with **rmdir**. Use the recursive remove command, **rm -r** *directory*, instead. **rm -r** will systematically remove all files and directories within and including *directory*. But remember, this command line should be used with utmost caution! For safety, habitually use the interactive option as in **rm -ir** *directory*.

PRACTICE!

> **10.** Copy your entire ~/Unix_work/Misc/ directory into ~/Unix_work/ Homework/.
>
> **11.** Remove the entire Misc/ directory inside ~/Unix_work/Homework/.

8.4.3 Quota

Many accounts place a *quota* on your account, or a limit on the amount of available memory for your files. To allow users to check account usage, many systems employ the **quota** *username* command:

STEP 85: CHECKING QUOTA

```
dis% quota dis                                    Check dis's account usage.

Filesystem   usage quota limit timeleft   files quota limit timeleft
/home/dis     9835 15000 15050             1085  2050  2100
```

Monitor the usage slot frequently. Usually, this quantity cannot exceed the quota slot.

The *disk use* command, **du -k**, also helps monitor memory usage. Enter **du -k ~** to display the memory consumed by your entire account.

8.4.4 Archiving

To save account space, create archives by "packing" important but infrequently used files into special directories. You can also pack particularly large files. Most Unix systems provide **compress** *file*, which will shrink, or *compress*, a file and rename it *filename*.**Z**. **uncompress** *file* will inflate the file to normal size. You may also encounter GNU's **gzip** compression. **gzip** appends gz instead of Z to the filename. Use **gzip** *file* to compress a file and **gzip -d** *file* to decompress a file. Investigate **zip**, too.

STEP 86: COMPRESS FILES

```
dis% vi big.txt                                Create a large text file, big.txt.

dis% ls -l big.txt              Long list the file, big.txt. My file is 115 bytes.

-rw-------  1  dis  ciegrad  115  Apr 30 23:37  big.txt

dis% compress big.txt                                    Shrink the text file.

dis% ls -l big.txt.Z          List the compressed file. My file shrunk to 45 bytes.

-rw-------  1  dis  ciegrad   45  Apr 30 23:45  big.txt.Z
```

Another compression command, **tar** (for *tape archiver*), packs files and directories together into a single file. Use **tar cvf *tarfile files*** to create a tar file from ***files*** ("**c**" for create, "**v**" for verbose mode, "**f**" to specify ***tarfile***. Supply the name, ***tarfile***, such as file.tar. The command line **tar cvf *tarfile* *** will tar everything in the current working directory. (The asterisk [*****] is a shortcut that will be discussed in the next section.) Use **tar xvf *tarfile*** to extract the contents of ***tarfile*** ("**x**" for extract). The command **tar tvf *tarfile*** displays a table of contents for ***tarfile*** ("**t**" for table of contents).

Also, check with your site about floppy disk storage. Typical commands involve **volcheck** or the **mtools** package, but these are system dependent. **volcheck** creates a directory called /floppy/ in which you can transfer files back and forth using Unix commands. **mtools** commands use MS-DOS format. Check with your system administrator for availability.

PRACTICE!

12. Store two text files, t1.txt and t2.txt, inside a directory ~/Unix_work/TEST/.
13. Tar the directory TEST/ into a file called test.tar.
14. Show the contents of test.tar.
15. Extract the contents from test.tar.
16. Delete the directory ~/Unix_work/TEST/.

8.5 MORE ABOUT SHELLS

Shell customization is important for extended Unix usage. Shortcuts, environment variables, and command aliases will all increase your efficiency and enhance your capability with Unix.

8.5.1 Shortcuts

Many shells allow shortcuts that substitute for filenames in certain situations. You have already used the tilde (~), a substitute for HOME. Recall that shells must interpret and translate command lines, so when the shell encounters predefined characters, it attempts to substitute appropriate filenames or pathnames.

Wildcards such as the asterisk or star (*****) assist in executing commands on groups of files at a time. Wildcards can substitute for any number of characters in a file or directory name. For example, use ***** to list everything in a directory that begins with the letter "t":

STEP 87:
WILDCARD
SUBSTITUTION

```
dis% cd ~/Unix_work/
```
Change CWD to Unix_work/ *subdirectory inside HOME.*

```
dis% ls t*
```
List any files and directories whose names start with the letter "t".

```
test1.txt test2.txt
```
These files were created in Section 8.2.

In general, you can use as many asterisks as you wish. For instance, enter **ls project*.*** to list all files starting with the name project and carrying any extension. To find hidden files with *****, precede them with the dot (.), as in **ls .*.**.

Other important wildcard characters include **?** and **[]**: the question mark (**?**) matches one character, while the square brackets (**[]**) to include a list of characters in your search:

<table>
<tr><td rowspan="3">**STEP 88:
CHARACTER
RANGE
SUBSTITUTION**</td><td>dis% **cd; mv test2.txt u2**</td><td>*Rename a text file.*</td></tr>
<tr><td>dis% **ls [tu]*?**</td><td>*Look for a file starting with* t *or* u *and ending with any single letter or number.*</td></tr>
<tr><td>test1.txt u2</td><td>*All files and directories matching the above criteria are listed.*</td></tr>
</table>

You can also find a range of letters or numbers with the square brackets. For instance, try **ls [a-c]*** for a listing of everything starting with a, b, or c.

The command **history** can save even more typing, as it produces a numbered list of recent command lines. Then, to execute one of them, you would type its number preceded by an exclamation point (!). Some systems employ the **fc** command instead of **history**. Some shells also "remember" a recent sequence of command lines, which you can review with the up arrow (↑) or **^P**. To move back down the list, use the down arrow (↓) or **^N**.

8.5.2 Variables

Shells contain local and global **variables** that affect command behavior. You have already studied variables such as HOME and PATH. Values assigned to variables instruct shells to interpret command lines in particular ways. For instance, returning to HOME with **cd** requires a HOME value such as /home/dis/.

Many programs require variable definitions stored in your system files. When logging in, your shell defines many variables for shell and session usage. Korn and Bourne Shells access the file variables housed in the file .profile inside a HOME directory. A Korn Shell also accesses .kshrc files whereas, the C Shell defines its variables with values from .login and .cshrc files. Other shells draw variables' values from similar files, which are known as *run-control* files. Two kinds of variables, local and global, affect your session.

Local, or **shell variables** affect shell behavior. For instance, the shell variable noclobber prevents overwriting of files. Inside .cshrc, then, you might find **set noclobber**, a command that instructs Unix not to overwrite files. (A .profile file defines the same variable with **set -o noclobber**.) These definitions are local, or specific, to the shell—within the same session, you could spawn shells with variables set to permit "clobbering." For C Shells, use lowercase letters when tinkering with shell variables. Enter **set** for a list of current shell variables. **unset *variable*** removes a definition.

Global, or **environment variables** affect your entire session and govern different programs requiring the same environment variables. For instance, my MAIL environment variable has the value /var/mail/dis, and a variety of programs, such as **netscape**, **elm**, **pine**, **emacs**, and **mailx**, incorporate and use MAIL. Use **setenv *VARIABLE value*** to assign environment variables in C Shells. Bourne and Korn Shells use the syntax ***VARIABLE=value***. Bourne and Korn users can also enter **set** or **env** for a full list of environment variables. C Shell users should enter **setenv** or **env** instead.

PRACTICE!

17. Call up a listing of all environment variables. Now, call up the value of just one environment variable from the list.

18. Create your own "ego" prompt. (Hint: check **man *shellname*.**)

8.5.3 Command Aliases

Remembering command options is difficult. Shells alleviate some of the strain by using command *aliases* or customized commands. For instance, why bother entering **ls -F** when you could use an alias to create a new command composed of **ls** and the **-F** option? Your new command, an alias for **ls -F**, might be named **lf**—or remain **ls** if you know that you will want the **-F** option invoked every time you enter **ls**.

Create aliases either in system files or at the command prompt. Korn Shells require the syntax **alias *new='old'***—be sure to use the single quote (**'**). Thus, **alias ls='ls -F'** redefines **ls** to automatically include the **-F** option while **alias lf='ls -F'** creates the new command **lf**. In both cases, the shell interprets the new command as **ls -F**. C Shells have a more liberated syntax in the creation of aliases. The same alias, **lf**, for example, could be defined with **alias lf ls -F** or **alias lf 'ls -F'**.

Regardless of shell, aliases create a personalized set of commands. For automatic loading each session, store aliases in system files. Enter **alias** to display a list of all defined aliases. Remove aliases with **unalias *command***, or use the backslash (\) character in the syntax ***command*** to temporarily turn off an aliased command.

PRACTICE!

> **19.** Create an alias for **ls** that lists all files along with types. Name the alias **ls**.
>
> **20.** Display your aliases. Now, remove your alias for **ls** and restore **ls** to its original funtion.

8.6 APPLICATION: SHARING YOUR WORK

In this section, you will set permissions for others to view and execute your **hello.C** program.

8.6.1 Problem

Your boss, Stuart, wants to try running your program without having to copy it into his account. He promises to give you a raise after he sees **Hello** in action. Also, your client is extremely pleased with your novel approach to producing the output **Hello World!**. D.I.S., Inc. is now contracted to expand this program to include a variety of features. Therefore, your team needs access to build other modules for the client.

8.6.2 Background

You need to assign file permissions such that others on your system can view and execute your work. However, you will not allow write permission in fear of accidental deletion.

8.6.3 Methodology

Use the command **ls -l** to learn more information on the files. The command **chmod** changes permissions. Do not forget to change permissions along the entire directory path! Consider also granting only execute permissions on everything unrelated to your **Hello** directory—unscrupulous coworkers might discover hidden rhyparography inside certain directories! (Nor would you want coworkers to put it there!)

8.6.4 Solution

Change your file and directory permissions with the following session.

STEP 89: CHANGING PERMISSIONS

```
dis% cd /home/    Change CWD to the parent of your HOME. (Also try doing this with cd ~/../.)

dis% ls -l                                    Check your account's permissions.

Some other users...            Your account should grant execute permission for group and world.
drwx--x--x  2  dis  team1  2560  Nov 1 9:25  dis
Some other users...        If you see drwxr-xr-x, enter chmod go-r dis for better protection.

dis% cd                                                 Change CWD to HOME.

dis% chmod a+rx PROJECTS/            Add read and execute permissions to PROJECTS/.

dis% chmod a+rx PROJECTS/Hello/        Add read and execute permissions to Hello/.

dis% chmod a+x Hello/HELLO          HELLO is an executable. Add execute permission.

dis% chmod a+r Hello/hello.C        Add read permission to your code file, hello.C.

dis% ls -alF PROJECTS/Hello/                    Check your file information.

drwxr-xr-x  2 dis team1  512 Oct 27 9:20 ./                    CWD.
drwxr-xr-x 17 dis team1 3072 Oct 27 9:08 ../          Parent of CWD.
-rwx--x--x  1 dis team1 8600 Oct 28 9:29 HELLO*           Executable.
-rw-r--r--  1 dis team1  181 Oct 28 9:25 hello.C                Code.
```

Congratulations! Stuart successfully executed your program and granted you a hefty raise. Aren't you glad that you used Unix?

SUMMARY

Advanced topics of the Unix operating system were introduced in this chapter. Unix offers a broad range of utilities for all tasks, and there are even other versions of Unix available to the Unix hobbyist for personal computing. Many advanced features involve file management and the Unix shell. Variables help define shell parameters: environment variables define settings and functions for your session, while shell variables affect specific shell behaviors. Both types of variables help customize the shell. Store customizations of commands as aliases inside system configuration files or at the command prompt.

APPLICATION: HOW TO DISCOVER MORE ABOUT UNIX

Unix is a fascinating subject that can draw you in and never let you go. Unix exudes mystery: At first, you experiment with simple commands. After all, what other choice do you have? But, scientists and engineers are an inquisitive lot. You wonder how other students have all those wild screen backgrounds and wonderful shell prompts.

Unix was designed to be discovered, and many people founded careers delving into its depths. To begin your own exploration, copy the run-control files from adept and knowledgeable users. Try to decipher each line of code in files such as .cshrc and .xinitrc. Also, study your site's literature, and maybe, buy a few computer books—they're relatively cheap and incredibly informative. Choose in particular books that discuss shells and shell programming. From shells, all else follows.

Manual pages also provide a wealth of knowledge. (Granted, manual pages are rather circular—knowing how to use **man** requires the command **man man**!) Try various command options described in the manual pages, then try customizing commands to automatically select options, as discussed in this chapter. Investigate related commands listed at the bottom of most manual pages—perhaps an unfamiliar command might ease your work.

In any case, manual pages supply complete options, syntax, and shell variables for Unix commands. Some of the most important of all manual pages concern the shell references. Try **man csh** or **man ksh** for rather lengthy, but extensive and helpful, manual pages. Try also **man -s 1 intro** and other section numbers—some systems completely list commands and descriptions in the intro pages.

Many will still choose to use Unix just because they have to. But computer-skill development, including competence with Unix, enhances your development in general as an engineer or scientist. Software is always in flux; new applications and techniques must be learned as technology improves. Knowing Unix will sharpen your ability to learn such new innovations and help you succeed throughout your career.

KEY TERMS

alias	GNU	variable
compress	Linux	wildcard
environment variable	quota	
file permission	shell variable	

Problems

1. Does your system support GNU software? If so, can you access these programs?

2. Where can you obtain a copy of Linux?

3. Demonstrate how you might compare the contents of two text files.

4. How would you view the last fifty lines of a text file?

5. How many words are there in your info.txt file?

6. How do you set the permissions drwxr-x--- for a directory called TEST/?

7. How do you set the permissions -rwxr-xr--? On what kind of item are you setting permissions?

8. Suppose that inside your HOME directory resides an item that **ls -F** outputs as bstein*. When you enter **ls -l**, you see the permissions -rw-------. What kind of item is bstein? Do these permissions help you use bstein*? If not, how would you change the permissions?

9. Create a file called foo.txt. Remove all user permissions for foo.txt. Can you now delete this file? If not, what should you do?

10. What options must you enter for **umask** to obtain permissions -rw------ on newly created files? (Hint: Try **man umask**.)

11. Create a subdirectory with the path ~/Unix_work/practice_tar/. Create five text files inside ~/Unix_work/practice_tar/. Tar these files into a single file called tar_test. Now, untar the files. Show all your command lines.

12. Remove the entire practice_tar/ subdirectory that you created in Problem 10. Use only one command line.

13. Determine your account quota and usage. Determine the top 5 memory-hogging files inside your account. Output your listing to a file as proof.

14. Research how to download to floppy disks on your system. Write a concise tip sheet with all important steps.

15. Display a list of currently assigned shell and environment variables. Show the names and values of at least five environment variables.

16. Create aliases for interactive **rm**, **cp**, and **mv** commands. Store these aliases inside an appropriate run-control file.

17. Project 1: Define all shell and environment variables inside your run-control files. (You should check manual pages for your shell for descriptions.) Present your report in three columns: variable name, assigned value, and description/role.

18. Project 2: Find ten commands not described in this text and write a synopsis for each. Include at least one example of usage.

19. Project 3: Create your own startup file for your system's shell. (Consult site literature and a book that contains information about shells.)

Appendix A
Symbol Names

!	exclamation point; bang	(	left parenthesis; open parenthesis
@	at sign	)	right parenthesis; close parenthesis
#	pound sign; sharp; hash	[	left square bracket
$	dollar sign	]	right square bracket
%	percent sign	{	left brace bracket; left curly brace
^	circumflex; caret	}	right brace bracket; right curly brace
&	ampersand; and	<	left angle bracket; less-than sign
°	asterisk; star	>	right angle bracket; greater-than sign
+	plus sign; add	/	forward slash; slash; virgule
=	equal sign	\	backslash; switch
~	tilde	:	colon
?	question mark; query	;	semicolon
|	vertical line; bar; pipe	`	back quotation mark; grave accent
_	underscore; underline	'	single quotation mark; apostrophe
-	hyphen; minus sign; dash	"	double quotation mark
,	comma	.	period; dot

Appendix B
Window Systems

B.1 TO GUI OR NOT TO GUI

In antediluvian[1] days, computer users relied on punch cards and teletype, but eventually, computer interfaces evolved to feature monochrome, "dumb" monitor terminals. Operating systems were designed for such text-based interfaces. Technology, though, has improved further, still. Graphical user interfaces (GUIs) provide an excellent medium for learning about and using computers. Nevertheless, underneath the graphical layer still lies the old text-based operating system.

Windows (and not just Bill Gates's variety) provide the interface between you and the operating system, accepting commands and running programs. However, windows can further shield a user from the operating system by replacing text-based command entry with point-and-click mouse operations. Unix window systems such as X Windows, Motif, and Common Desktop Environment (CDE) provide graphical, mouse-based interfaces to initate applications. In this appendix, fundamentals of GUIs are reviewed.

B.2 GUI BASICS

Using a GUI requires an understanding of mouse input, window operations, and workspace management.

B.2.1 Mouse

The mouse helps control and guide navigation through your windows. A typical Unix mouse has three buttons, as illustrated in Figure B.1. You perform three basic operations your mouse: pressing buttons, releasing buttons, and moving the cursor. All other mouse operations are conducted via those operations:

- *Click*: Press and release a button, usually within a one- to two-second time span.
- *Double-click*: Rapidly click the same button twice.
- *Point*: Move the mouse with your right hand until the mouse icon on the monitor screen (often an arrow) touches the desired image.
- *Grab*: Point the mouse to a graphical image, and press and hold the left button.
- *Drag*: Grab an image, and while still holding the left button down, move the mouse.

B.2.2 Window

The monitor's screen is a *workspace*. *Windows* reside inside the workspace, as shown in Figure B.1. Consult local system literature for choosing a GUI when logging on.

---

[1] "Before the Great Flood"; i.e., long ago.

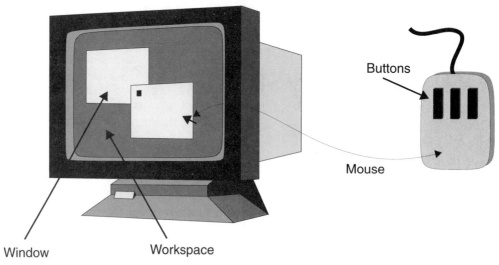

Figure B.1.   Basic GUI Components

Sometimes a few windows are opened by default when you log on. Important features common to windows are displayed in Figure B.2. The terminal window pictured in Figure B.2 is a program called **dtterm**, which is in CDE. Other common windows programs include **xterm**, **shelltool**, and **cmdtool**. Such windows programs provide text-based interfaces for Unix commands. You can open these windows by entering a command such as **xterm &** or selecting a menu option.

Be sure to adapt your mouse actions to your system's configurations: depending on the system, you might have to press right or middle mouse buttons instead of left. Common window operations include:

- *Selecting*: Point the mouse somewhere on the window to pull that window to the foreground. Sometimes you have to click once with the left button.
- *Moving*: Moving windows is akin to shuffling papers on a desk. Point the mouse on the window's title bar. Now, drag the window.
- *Choosing Menu Items*: Point to and press your left mouse button on **Window** and other items in the menu bar. Don't let go of the button! More choices will appear on a pulldown menu. Now, still holding down the mouse button, select one item by pointing your mouse at the item and then releasing the button.
- *Resizing*: Point the mouse at any border or corner. Press and drag the border of the window, releasing the button when you are satisfied with the size. (Try the window operations menu for other resizing options.)
- *Raising/Lowering*: When windows are stacked, there can be only one "on top," usually the active, or foreground, one. *Raising* pushes a window higher in a stack. Raise a window by clicking once on the title bar or by choosing the **Raise** menu option. *Lowering* moves a window lower in the stack.
- *Iconifying*: Iconifying, or minimizing, reduces the window to a small icon elsewhere on the screen. Minimizing might also store your window in an on-screen box called a *window manager*.
- *Maximizing*: This operation enlarges your window to occupy the full area of the monitor screen.

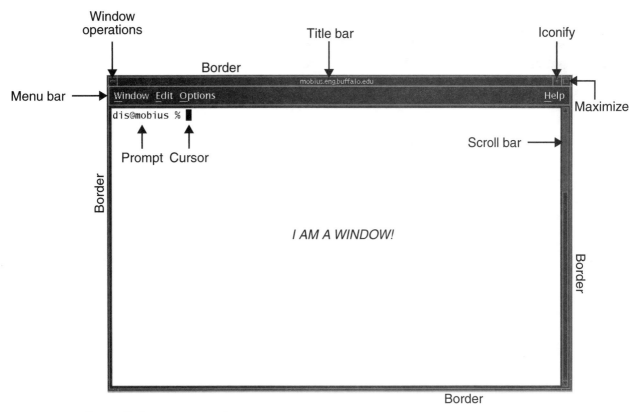

Figure B.2. `dtterm` Window

- *Closing:* Also called *destroying, closing* kills a window and all of its processes. The window is erased from your workspace, never to return. (Remember: Even if you close a window, you have not logged out until exiting the *entire* GUI!)

B.2.3 Cursor

Often will you enter commands in a *terminal window* on the screen. These windows act like little monitors that accept text-based command entry. As discussed, sometimes you must point and click your mouse to activate a window. An *active* window accepts keyboard input. Sometimes a blinking cursor helps identify the active window. Setting **Autofocus** tells your system to accept keyboard input wherever your mouse points.

B.2.4 Workspace

Imagine that you could simultaneously log on to four different computers with just one login—*workspaces* achieve the same effect. You can switch back and forth to different screens, or workspaces, on the same monitor. You may assign different collections of windows, all running applications, in each workspace. Many windows-systems now support this feature.

B.2.5 Applications

Often, the GUI bundles applications such as e-mail, printing, and on-line help. CDE, for instance, supplies the Front Panel application reproduced in Figure B.3. The front panel provides a variety of features: from it you can choose different menus and select

Figure B.3. CDE Front Panel

applications, which open new windows. Press one of the middle buttons on Front Panel such as **One** or **Two** to change your workspace.

B.3 PROCESSES

GUIs are multitasking: each window and subsequent process adds to the collection of processes running during your session. Needless to say, then, GUIs require significant computer memory. However, process management is simplified with a GUI—if you dislike an errant process, simply destroy the window and free up memory. Run your window-based programs from terminal windows. Append an ampersand (&) to commands to send them to the background. For instance, entering `xman &` sends the `xman` process into the background and frees the terminal window for further command entry. Look inside `/util/X11/bin/` and `/util/dt/bin/` directories for many windows-based programs.

B.4 LOGGING OUT

Exiting a single terminal or console window typically will not log you out—you must tell your interface that you are quitting. Look for **exit** or **quit** menu options, then wait until the login prompt reappears just to be safe.

Now, go have fun!

Appendix C
Text Editors

C.1 PICO

If you are inexperienced with text editors, use **pico**. To activate, enter the command line **pico**. To load or create a specific file, use **pico** *filename*. More command line options are described in **man pico**.

C.1.1 Using **pico**

Enter text in **pico** as you would in any other Unix situation, by typing in the text. To move from line to line in your text, use the up and down arrow keys. To edit, use the **^Key** commands, such as those listed at the bottom of the screen. Practice these commands by cutting a line of text. First, move the cursor to the beginning of the line and enter **^K**. Now, to paste the line elsewhere, move the cursor to where you want to place the text and press **^U**. The Get Help command, **^G**, will reveal more information.

C.1.2 Saving and Exiting

Occasionally, save your work with **^O**, which "writes out" your data to a file. **pico** will prompt, "File Name to write : ", as shown in Figure C.2. Enter a name and then continue editing. When you finish editing, press **^X**. If you have not already saved your work, **pico** will now prompt you to do so and ask for a filename if you did not originally specify one.

C.2 EMACS

emacs belongs to the GNU distribution of Unix and is therefore not standard to all versions. However, many systems do carry the software, which you start by entering **emacs**

Figure C.1. The **pico** Text Editor

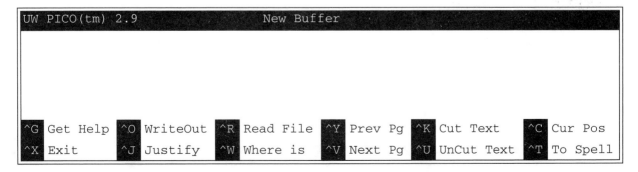

```
UW PICO(tm) 2.9                    New Buffer                      Modified
You enter text here.
You can enter even more text here.
How about another line?
Now enter ^O to save this "buffer" to a file.



File Name to write : enter filename here
^G Get Help   ^T  To Files
^C Cancel     TAB Complete
```

Figure C.2. Saving Your Work with **pico**

or **emacs *options filename***. A typical **emacs** session screen is shown in Figure C.3.

C.2.1 Key Sequences

Commands in **emacs** generally involve control-key or meta-key sequences, indicated as C-key and M-key respectively in **emacs** notation. For Control commands, press and *hold* **Control** and then hit **key**. For M-key sequences, hit the Meta key, hold it, and then press **key**. On many systems, the **Esc** key acts as Meta, but other systems employ **Alt** instead, and still others, such as Sun, use ◆ for **Meta**. When using **Esc**, press and release it, and do not hold it when pressing **key**.

C.2.2 Basic Commands

emacs starts in fundamental mode, and other modes are available for different applications, such as help and mail. Each mode has unique commands. For an on-line tutorial, enter **C-h t**(that is, **^H-t**). Also, try **Meta-x** followed by Spacebar to see a complete listing of available commands. Some basic **emacs** commands are listed in Table C-1— beware that **emacs** is case-sensitive!

Figure C.3. The **emacs** Text Editor

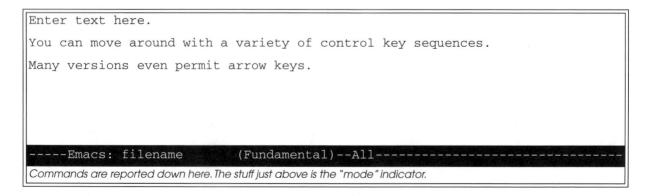

```
Enter text here.
You can move around with a variety of control key sequences.
Many versions even permit arrow keys.




-----Emacs: filename        (Fundamental)--All-------------------------------
Commands are reported down here. The stuff just above is the "mode" indicator.
```

TABLE C-1 emacs Commands

COMMAND	DESCRIPTION
C-p	Move up one line
C-n	Move down one line
C-f	Move forward one character
C-b	Move backward one character
M-v	Move up one page
C-v	Move down one page
M-<	Move to top of document
M->	Move to bottom of document
C-d	Delete one character to the right
C-k	Cut one line of text
C-y	Paste ("yank") anything that was just cut
C-g	Interrupt an input command
C-x u	Undo the most recent change
C-h	Find help
C-x C-s	Save your work
C-x C-w	Write the file contents to another file
C-x C-c	Exit **emacs**

Appendix D
E-mail Programs

D.1 ELM

elm is a popular text-based, menu-driven e-mail program. If available on your system, activate it with the command **elm**. First-time users will be requested to create .elm/ and Mail/ directories. A typical **elm** window is displayed in Figure D.1: The top line shows your system mailbox which stores incoming mail. Commands are entered at the bottom using the listed menu options.

Unread, or "new," messages are indicated by the "N" on their left. The current message being viewed is typically highlighted in the mailbox bar, as shown below. Select the curent message using the arrow keys (↓ and ↑), or menu options **j** and **k**, and press **Return** to read it. Be careful *not* to press **Return** after entering menu commands.

D.2 PINE

pine is another user-friendly program that uses many one-letter commands. After entering the command **pine**, you are placed inside the main menu, shown in Figure D.2. The commands shown there can be entered from main menu as well as from almost everywhere else in **pine**. Other commands are listed at the bottom of the window. Do not press **Return** after typing these and many other **pine** commands!

Figure D.1. `elm`

```
            Mailbox is '/var/mail/dis' with 3 messages [ELM 2.4 PL25]


  N  1   Nov 27 Ben Stein          (75)    Charm Tape on its way

  N  2   Nov 28 Chester Zeshonski  (26)    New Metallica
  N  3   Nov 29 Eugene Demaitre    (30)    E.A.D.2D.I.S.11/29/97D




    You can use any of the following commands by pressing the first character;
   d)elete or u)ndelete mail,  m)ail a message,  r)eply or f)orward mail,  q)uit
      To read a message, press <return>.  j = move down, k = move up, ? = help
```

```
PINE 3.96    MAIN MENU                        Folder: INBOX   2 Messages


        ?     HELP                  -  Get help using Pine
        C     COMPOSE MESSAGE       -  Compose and send/post a message
        I     FOLDER INDEX          -  View messages in current folder
        L     FOLDER LIST           -  Select a folder OR news group
        A     ADDRESS BOOK          -  Update address book
        S     SETUP                 -  Configure or update Pine
        Q     QUIT                  -  Exit the Pine program


     Copyright 1989-1997. PINE is a trademark of the University of Washington.

? Help                    P PrevCmd                 R RelNotes
O OTHER CMDS L [ListFldrs] N NextCmd
```

Figure D.2. **pine**'s Main Menu

D.2.1 Reading E-mail

Mail programs make extensive use of folders, files or directories that store e-mail. In **pine**, folders are found by selecting **L** from the main menu. All incoming e-mail is stored in an INBOX, the new-mail folder displayed in Figure D.3. The INBOX may be accessed by entering **I**. Select and read messages from this or any other folder by moving the arrow keys up and down to highlight the desired message, then pressing **Return**.

D.2.2 Composing E-mail

Select **C** to compose a message—a window similar to that in Figure D.4 will open, and you will be prompted to enter the message headers. Use the arrow keys to move up and down through the window. Move past the Message Text line to write and edit the

Figure D.3. **pine**'s INBOX Folder

```
   PINE 3.96    FOLDER INDEX              Folder: INBOX  Message 1 of 3 NEW


+  N      1 Nov 24 Rogil Camama        (982)    Re: kind of like last weekend
+  N      2 Now 25 Al Somlo            (830)    FREE Mobius site updates
+  N      3 Nov 26 Jeff Chottiner      (1,220)  Interview




? Help          M Main Menu  P PrevMsg  -   PrevPage  D Delete    R Reply
O OTHER CMDS    V [ViewMsg]  N NextMsg  Spc NextPage  U Undelete  F Forward
```

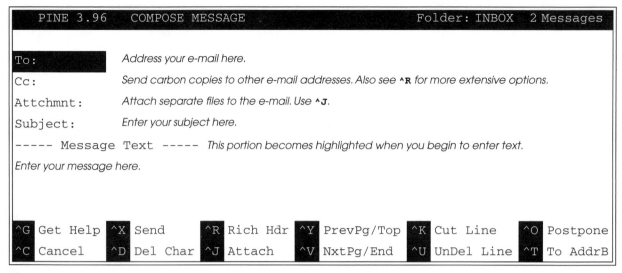

Figure D.4. Sending Mail

body of your e-mail. Commands to assist your editing will appear at the bottom of the window. When finished editing, enter **^X** to send the message. Note that **^X** is interactive, so you will be asked to confirm that you want to send the message. Remember not to press **Return** after these key strokes.

D.2.3 Quitting

Enter **Q** to quit **pine**. Don't fear a mysterious "expunge" question—all **pine** wants to know is whether you prefer to remove previously read messages from the INBOX. If you have configured **pine** to automatically move read messages, **pine** will store these messages in another folder, usually called read-messages inside ~/mail/.

Both **pine** and **elm** have many more features. Definitely experiment with both programs when the opportunity arises.

Appendix E
Suggested Web Resources

The following are some World Wide Web pages that you might find useful—for Unix and otherwise.

Dictionaries

http://www.m-w.com
http://www2.dictionary.com/dictionary

Computer History and Unix

http://www.UNIX-systems.org
http://www.chac.org/chac/chhistpg.html

Unix Alternatives

http://www.gnu.org
http://www.linux.org

On-line Unix Help

http://www.geek-girl.com/unix.html

Carpal Tunnel Syndrome

http://www.cs.princeton.edu/~dwallach/tifaq
http://www.stretching.com

Virtual Reality

http://wings.buffalo.edu/academic/department/eng/mae/vrlab
http://www.vrml.org

Pattern Recognition

http://www.cedar.buffalo.edu

Unicode

http://www.unicode.org

Stone SouperComputer

http://www.esd.ornl.gov/facilities/beowulf/

Qualitative Physics

http://ai-www.aist-nara.ac.jp/doc/qphysics
http://www.cs.utexas.edu/users/qr

Java

http://www.java.org
http://www.sun.com

The Internet

http://www.internic.net
http://www.isi.edu/iab
http://www.isoc.org

File Transfer Protocol (FTP) Sites

http://hoohoo.ncsa.uiuc.edu/ftp/
http://www.iaehv.nl/users/perry/ftp-list.html

Netiquette

http://www.fau.edu:80/rinaldi/netiquette.html
http://www.cybernothing.org/faqs/net-abuse-faq.html
http://wings.buffalo.edu/computing/policies/use.html

Complete Solutions to Practice Problems

Chapter 2: Sample Unix Session

1. "^" is called *caret* and *circumflex*.
2. "-" is called *hyphen* and *minus sign*.
3. "**am i**" is not a proper command line.
4. "**WHO AM I**" causes an error message to be displayed.
5. Enter **echo $SHELL** to find out the default system shell.
6. Entering **echo SHELL** gives as output the word SHELL.
7. Enter **exit**. You might have to exit your GUI to log out.
8. Wait for login prompt; repeat the login procedure.
9. **logout** may not be understood by your shell.

Chapter 3: File Editing

1. 1024 characters = 1024 bytes = 1 kilobyte.
2. Nineteen bytes (be sure to count spaces.) Make that 20 if the end of the line includes **Return**. (There are ASCII characters for "new line" and other text operations.)
3. Yes, project#1_b.txt is an acceptable filename, because all the characters are acceptable for use in Unix filenames. In general, though, you ought to avoid the pound sign character (#).
4. **vi test.txt**.
5. "test.txt" [New file]. You are in command mode.
6. Use input mode commands such as **i**.
7. Press **Esc**. Next, enter the characters **:wq** followed by **Return**. You enter **wq** to first save your work and then quit **vi**.
8. **vi info.txt**.
9. Use input mode commands. Don't forget to save and quit when you are finished.
10. **:wq**.
11. **vi big.txt**.
12. Toggle to input mode with **i**.
13. Edit the file with **vi**, display with **more**, or list with **ls**.
14. **more** displays --More--(*percentage*). The percentage corresponds to the amount of the file that you have viewed so far. Type **q** to quit.
15. **vi new.txt**.
16. Use insert mode and start typing.

17. Try either **echo $LPDEST** or **echo $PRINTER**.
18. Use **lp new.txt** for the default printer.
    Use **lp -d** *printer_name* **new.txt** for a specific printer.
19. You know that a file has been printed when **lpstat** no longer lists the job. (You will certainly know when you obtain the actual printout.)

Chapter 4: Communication and the Internet

1. **cal** displays a calendar. Try **cal 12 2067**: December 16, 2067, is a Friday.
2. **finger -m** *username* shows real name, HOME directory, last login, shell, new mail, and maybe a "plan" file.
3. **mailx** *username*.
4. **mailx** *username1 username2*.
5. **mailx** *username* **< info.txt**.
6. Enter **mailx**. Enter the message number corresponding to test2. Then, enter **s test2.txt**.
7. At the prompt, enter the following, hitting **Return** after each:
   1. **ftp explorer.arc.nasa.gov**.
   2. **cd /pub/space/GIFS/**.
   3. **ls**.
   4. **binary**.
   5. **get** *filename*.
   6. **bye**.
8. At the prompt, enter the following, hitting **Return** after each.
   1. **ftp rtfm.mit.edu**.
   2. **cd /pub/usenet-by-group/news.answers/engineering**.
   3. **get pe-eit-exam**.
   4. **bye**.
9. www.asce.org corresponds to the American Society of Civil Engineers (ASCE) Web site.
10. Enter **ftp://rtfm.mit.edu** into your Web browser. In succession click on pub/, usenet-by-group/, news.answers/, faqs/, about-faqs. Use the Save option in the File menu to download the file. (For a quicker method, visit http://www.faqs.org/faqs/faqs/about-faqs.)
11. No, URLs must include both a method and a location. Browsers usually compensate for omissions of method by appending one for you—try entering just **www.aaes.org** without the **http://** portion.

Chapter 5: Directories

1. /home/dis/info.txt.
2. /home/chz/.
3. info.txt.
4. Use **echo $HOME** to answer.
5. Root is the parent of all directories. Therefore, root contains all HOME directories. If home/ is the directory that contains HOME, HOME is the child of home/.

6. `/home/`. (Your system might have a different configuration.)
7. Double dot (`..`) only.
8. **cd ~**: Change CWD to HOME.
9. **cd ~/**: Change CWD to HOME.
10. **cd ~dis**: Change CWD to HOME directory of user `dis`.
11. **cd ~/dis/**: Change CWD to a subdirectory called `dis/` inside *your* HOME.
12. **cd**.
13. **ls**. Use **mkdir ~/Unix_work/** to create the subdirectory if it does not exist.
14. First, enter **cd Unix_work/**. Then, enter **cd**.
15. **mkdir ~/Unix_work/Misc/**. You could also enter **cd Unix_work/**, followed by **mkdir Misc/**.
16. **cd ~/Unix_work/Misc/**.
17. Enter **cd**, then **ls Unix_work/**.
18. **mkdir ~/Unix_work/Test2/**.
19. **cd ~/Unix_work/Test2/**.
20. Enter **cd ..** followed by **rmdir Test2/**.

Chapter 6: File Management

1. Enter **cd**, then **ls -F**.
2. First, **vi .delete_me**. Add some lines of text and exit. Next, enter **ls -a** in HOME. Finally, use **more .delete_me** to display the file.
3. **ls -F Unix_work/Misc/**.
4. Enter **more info.txt**, then **more info2.txt**. (**more info.txt info2.txt** will also work.)
5. The files are identical because **cp** makes a duplicate, and **mv** renames the same file.
6. **rm ~/big.txt** and **rm ~/test.txt**.
7. **ls ~**.
8. So far, you have been working in HOME.
9. Use **cp info.txt Unix_work/Misc/info.txt** or **cp info.txt Unix_work/Misc/** to apply relative pathnames.
10. Confirm the backup with **more Unix_work/Misc/info.txt**.
    Delete the original with **rm ~/info.txt**.
11. **mkdir ~/Unix_work/Misc/DELETE_ME/**.
12. **cd ~/Unix_work/Misc/DELETE_ME/**.
13. Try relative pathnames in the command line **cp ../info.txt ../info_copy.txt**. Here, double dot (`..`) refers to the parent directory, `Misc/`.
14. This one is tricky—you are copying a file *into* the CWD. Remember that dot (`.`) represents the CWD. Thus, the new pathname is just dot (`.`) for **mv**. Use the command line **mv ../info_copy.txt ./**.
    (Translation: Move the file `info_copy.txt` from its parent directory into the current working directory.)
15. First, delete the file `info_copy.txt`, using **rm info_copy.txt**. Then, change your CWD using **cd ..**, and lastly, remove the directory with **rmdir DELETE_ME/**.

Chapter 7: Unix Tools and Utilities

1. **ls** = command, **-a** = option, **/home/jchottin/** = argument.
2. Yes, Unix can understand more than one blank space. However, do not enter spaces between dashes and option names!
3. Yes, **lp -md *printer file*** is acceptable: the option **-m** does not take arguments, but **-d** does.
4. Enter **cd**, then **ls < ./**, **ls < ~/**, or **ls < ~*username***. Redirecting input produces the same output as entering **ls** alone.
5. **ls ~/Unix_work/Misc/ > home_list.txt**.
6. **cd ; ls**.
7. **ls -R ~ | more**.
8. The command line **ls > list.txt ; more list.txt** stores the CWD listing in list.txt, after which the file is displayed. The command line **ls | more** pipes the CWD listing into **more**. The second method is certainly more elegant and convenient.
9. Check the pathname using **which mv**. If you get an "aliased" message, try **which \mv**. If your system doesn't know **which**, try **whence -p** or **type**.
10. Use **ls -F *pathname*/mv**: A star (*) indicates that **mv** is a binary file.
11. Most of the time, you can enter **pwd**. Use **type pwd** to find the path. If the path is /usr/bin, enter **/usr/bin/pwd** for the second method.
12. Your **/home/~*username*/Unix_work/** directory is not an executable file.
13. Use **man ls**.
14. Use **ls -x** to sort horizontally.
15. Enter **man man** for discussion of the **-k** option. **man -k *keyword*** searches your system for commands that have ***keyword*** in the name or description. Thus, **man -k browse** finds a list of commands that somehow contain the word *browse*.
16. Enter **man -s 3 intro**. This intro page offers a listing of C functions.
17. **finger ira > ira.txt &**.
18. **ps ; jobs**.
19. **fg %1**.
20. **stop %1; kill %1**. Check to see if ira.txt still exists—these commands won't work if Unix is already finished with the process.

Chapter 8: Advanced Unix

1. **banner *username* > me.txt**.
2. **spell test1.txt**.
3. The directory Unix_work/ grants read, write, and execute permission only to the owner, dis. Thus, only the owner can list, modify, or access Unix_work/.
4. The file test1.txt has read and write permissions for the owner, dis. Any groups dis belongs to have only read permission. All other permissions are restricted. Thus, dis and his groups can view and copy test1.txt, but only dis can edit the file.
5. dis's HOME directory must have either read or execute permissions. Otherwise, groups would not be able to access the file, /home/dis/text1.txt.

6. The file permissions drrxrrxrrx are nonsensical for any file. Each collection of fields must follow the pattern rwx. Although a dash (–) may be substituted for any field, the pattern rwx must still be followed.

7. **cd ; cd ../ ; ls -l**.

   Look for the listing corresponding to your username.

8. Enter **chmod go-r username** if the CWD is /home/. Otherwise, enter **chmod go-r ~username**.

9. Accessible HOME directory: **chmod a+x ~username**.

   No listing on Home: **chmod go-r ~username**.

   Long listing for HOME: **ls -al /home/ | more**.

   Unix_work/ directory: **chmod a+rx ~/Unix_work/**.

   Long listing for Unix_work/: **ls -al ~/ | more**.

10. **cd ~/Unix_work/ ; ls**.

    cp -r Misc/ Homework/ ; ls ; ls Homework/.

11. **cd Homework/ ; rm -ir Misc/ ; ls**.

12. **mkdir ~/Unix_work/TEST/ ; vi t1.txt ; vi t2.txt**.

13. **tar cvf test.tar ~/Unix_work/TEST/**.

14. **tar tvf test.tar**.

15. **tar xvf test.tar**.

16. **rm -r ~/Unix_work/TEST/**.

17. **env ; echo $VISUAL**.

18. For C Shells, use **set prompt=username%**. Bourne and Korn Shell users should try **PS1=username$**. You may wish to enter a blank space after the last character % or $.

19. C Shell users enter **alias ls 'ls -aF'** or **alias ls ls -af'**.

    Korn Shell users enter **alias ls='ls -aF'**.

20. **env ; unalias ls**.

COMMAND SUMMARY

- Commands are shown in **bold**.
- Command options are listed in square brackets ([ ]). Do not type these. Check manual pages for more options.
- Command arguments are shown in ***bold italic***. Do not type the name of the argument; type the *value* of the argument!

COMMAND SYNTAX	DESCRIPTION	EXAMPLES	SECTION(S)
alias	Show list of all command aliases	**alias**	8.5
alias ***mycommand commandline***	Define a command alias (C Shell)	**alias rm rm -i**	
alias ***mycommand='commandline'***	Define a command alias (Korn Shell)	**alias rm='rm -i'**	
bg [***%process_id***]	Place the most recent process suspended in the background	**bg**	7.6
	Place a specific process in the background	**bg %1**	
cancel [***%request_id***]	Cancel the most recent print job	**cancel**	3.5
	Cancel a specific print job	**cancel ntx-1216**	
cat ***files***	Display one text file	**cat file1**	7.3, 7.6, 8.2
	Display text files in succession by concatenating them	**cat file1 file2**	
	Create a text file	**cat > file1**	
cd ***directory***	Change working directory	**cd ~/Unix_work/**	5.3, 5.4, 6.4
compress ***file***	Compress a file	**compress big.ps**	8.4
cp [***-ir***] ***source target***	Place a copy of source in destination	**cp file1 file2**	6.2, 6.3, 6.4, 8.4
-i	Interactive copy (prompt user for **y** or **n**)	**cp -i ~dis/hw1.ps ~/HW/**	
-r	Recursive copy (copy entire directories)	**cp -r dir1 dir2**	
chmod [***ugoa***] [***+-***] [***rwx***] ***file***	Change access permissions	**chmod a+r /home/dis/**	8.3
		chmod a-rx ~/Unix_work/	
		chmod g+r test.txt	
date	Display the date and time	**date**	4.3
du [***-k***] ***directory***	Show disk usage	**du**	8.4
-k	Show file sizes in kilobytes	**du -k ~/**	
echo	Echo text input	**echo HELLO**	2.3, 5.2, 7.4
	Echo variable value	**echo $HOME**	
elm	Send and read e-mail	**elm**	App. D
emacs [***file***]	Start the **emacs** text editor, edit/create file	**emacs**	App. C
		emacs test.txt	
env	Display all environment variable assignments	**env**	8.5
exit	Exit a shell; can sometimes log out	**exit**	2.3
fg [***%process_id***]	Place the most recent process in the foreground	**fg**	7.6
	Place a specific process in the foreground	**fg %1**	

continued on next page

COMMAND SYNTAX	DESCRIPTION	EXAMPLES	SECTION(S)
`finger` `[-m]``[name]`     `-m`	Show information about who's using the system Locate information about users Locate information about a particular username	`finger` `finger dave` `finger -m dis`	4.3
`ftp` `[ftpsite]`	Transfer file across computer hosts and the Internet	`ftp` `ftp ftp.eng.buffalo.edu`	4.5
`grep` `string files`	Search for text strings in files and directories	`grep Hello! *.txt`	8.2
`host` `hostname`	Find IP addresses	`host whitehouse.gov`	4.2
`jobs`	List pending and suspended process	`jobs`	7.6

`kill` `[-9]` `PID`
    `-9`
`kill` `[%process_id]`
	Kill a process using the PID number (see **ps**)
	    Obliterate all processes associated with PID
	Kill a process using the ID listed by the job
	shell (see **jobs**)
		`kill 1234`
		`kill -9 1234`
		`kill %1`
			7.6

`listusers`	Shows users with system access	`listusers`	4.3, 7.6

`lp` `[-m]` `[-d printer]` `file`
    `-d`
    `-m`
	Print a file
	    Print a file at specific printer
	    Print a file and send e-mail when finished
		`lp text.dat`
		`lp -d printer6 *.ps`
		`lp -m text.dat`
			3.5, 3.6, 7.3

`lpstat`	Check on print-job status	`lpstat`	3.5, 3.6

`ls` `[-aFlR]` `[pathname]`
 	
    `-a`
 	
    `-F`
    `-l`
 	
    `-R`
	List the contents of a directory; can also list
	individual files
	List all the contents of a directory including
	hidden files
	List contents and file types of a directory
	List all information about the contents
	of a directory
	Recursively list the contents
	    of a subdirectory
		`ls`
		
		`ls -a .*`
		
		`ls -F Unix_work/`
		`ls -l project.*`
		
		`ls -Ral ~/`
			3.4, 5.3, 5.4, 6.1,
			6.2, 7.3, 7.7, 8.3

`mailx` `[username]`	Read e-mail and access **mailx** commands
	Send e-mail
	Mail a file
		`mailx`
		`mailx dis`
		`mailx dorris < free.txt`
			4.4, 4.6

`man` `[-s section]` `commandname`
    `-s`
	Display manual page
	    Display the manual page from a specific section
		`man ls`
		`man -s 1 intro`
			7.5, 7.7

`mesg` `[ny]`
    `n`
    `y`
	Check status of **mesg**
	    Deny message requests from other users
	    Accept message requests from other users
		`mesg`
		`mesg n`
		`mess y`
			4.3

`mkdir` `directory`	Create a subdirectory	`mkdir MOBIUS/`	5.4, 5.5, 6.3
`more` `file`	Display a text file	`more chattin.txt`	3.4, 3.6, 6.4, 7.3, 7.4

`mv` `[-i]` `source target`
    `-i`
	Rename or move directories and files.
	    Interactive move (prompt for **y** or **n**)
		`mv apples.txt fruit/`
		`mv -i fruit/ FRUIT/`
			6.2, 6.3, 6.4, 8.4

`news` `[-s]`
    `-s`
	Show system news
	    Display how many news items have
	    accumulated
		`news`
		`news -s`
			4.3

`passwd`	Change your password	`passwd`	2.5
`pico` `[file]`	Edit a text file with **pico**	`pico` `pico ml.txt`	App. C
`pine`	Send and read e-mail using pine	`pine`	App. D

`ps` `[-ef]` `[-u username]`
    `-e`
    `-f`
    `-u`
	List processes
	    List all processes
	    List processes in full format
	    List processes for a particular user
		`ps`
		`ps -f`
		`ps -ef`
		`ps -fu dis`
			7.6

`pwd`	Display current working directory	`pwd`	5.3, 5.4

`quota` `[username]`
    `-v`
	Display system memory usage
	    Display usage on all accessible systems
		`quota`
		`quota -v`
			8.4

continued on next page

COMMAND SYNTAX	DESCRIPTION	EXAMPLES	SECTION(S)
`rm` `[-ir]` *pathname*	Remove a file	`rm junk.txt`	6.2, 6.3, 6.4, 8.4
`-i`	Interactive remove (prompt for **y** or **n**)	`rm -i junk.txt`	
`-r`	Recursively remove all files and directories	`rm -ri JUNK/`	
`rmdir` *directory*	Remove empty subdirectory	`rmdir temp/`	5.4, 6.3
`set` `[`*variable*`]`	Show list current shell variables	`set`	8.5
	Assign a local shell variable	`set noclobber`	
`setenv` `[`*VARIABLE*`]` `[`*value*`]`	Show list of environment variables (C Shells)	`setenv`	8.5
	Assign a global, environment variable (C Shells)	`setenv EDITOR emacs`	
`stop` `[`*%process_id*`]`	Suspend a process	`stop %1`	7.6
`talk` *username*`[`*@hostname*`]`	Chat on-line with another user	`talk ds5`	4.3
`tar` `[ctx]` `[vf]` *tarfile files*	Pack files directories together into a single file		8.4
`c`	Create a tar file	`tar cvf data.tar *.*`	
`t`	Show table of contents in tar file	`tar tvf data.tar`	
`x`	Extract all contents of the tar file	`tar xvf data.tar`	
`telnet` `[`*host*`]`	Remotely access another computer host	`telnet` `telnet free.org`	4.5
`type` *command*	Show information about Unix commands	`type ls`	7.4
`unalias` *command*	Remove any aliases associated with *command*	`unalias mv`	8.5
`uncompress` *file*	Uncompress a file	`uncompress big.ps.Z`	8.4
`vi` `[`*file*`]`	Edit text with `vi`	`vi` `vi test.txt`	3.2, 3.3, 3.6
`who` `[am i]`	Show list of users currently logged on	`who`	2.3, 4.3
`am i`	Report information about yourself	`who am i`	

Bibliography

Unix History
Salus, Peter H. *A Quarter Century of Unix*. Reading, Mass.: Addison-Wesley, 1994.

Carpal Tunnel Syndrome and Stretching
Anderson, Bob. *Stretching at Your Computer or Desk*. Bolinas, Calif.: Shelter Publications, 1996.

Unix Tutorials
Afzal, Amir. *Unix Unbounded: A Beginning Approach*. Upper Saddle River, N.J.: Prentice Hall, 1998.

Reichard, Kevin, and Eric F. Johnson. *Teach Yourself Unix*. New York: MIS: Press, 1995.

Unix References
Gilly, Daniel, and the staff of O'Reilly and Associates, Inc. *Unix in a Nutshell*. Sebastopol, Calif.: O'Reilly & Associates, 1992.

Reichard, Kevin, and Eric Foster-Johnson. *Unix in Plain English*. New York: MIS: Press, 1997.

Rosen, Kenneth H., Richard R. Rosinski, James M. Farber, and Douglas A. Host. *Unix System V Release 4: An Introduction*. 2nd ed. Berkeley, Calif.: McGraw-Hill, 1996.

Trademarks

"AIX" is a trademark of the International Business Machines Corporation.

"AT&T" and "System V" are registered trademarks of AT&T.

"Berkeley Software Distribution" and "BSD" are trademarks of the Regents of University of California at Berkeley.

"GIF" is a service mark property of CompuServe, Inc.

"GNU", "GNU Emacs" and "Emacs" are trademarks of the Free Software Foundation.

"Hewlett Packard" and "HP-UX" are trademarks of Hewlett Packard Company.

"IRIX" and "Silicon Graphics" are trademarks of Silicon Graphics, Inc.

"Java", "Solaris", "Sun", and "SunOS" are trademarks of Sun Microsystems, Inc.

"Linux" is a registered trademark of Linus Torvalds.

"MS-DOS" is a trademark of Microsoft, Inc.

"Netscape Navigator" is a trademark of the Netscape Communications Corporation.

"OSF", "Motif", "Unix", and "X/Open" are registered trademarks of the Open Group.

"Pico" and "Pine" are trademarks of the University of Washington.

"PostScript" is a registered trademark of Adobe Systems, Inc.

"Unicode" is a registered trademark of Unicode, Inc.

"X Windows" is a trademark of the Massachusetts Institute of Technology, Inc.

"XENIX", "SCO Unix", and "UnixWare" are registered trademarks of the Santa Cruz Operation.

Other product and company names that are mentioned herein may be the trademarks of their respective owners.

Index

STEPS